THE NEW MERMAIDS

The Revenger's Tragedy

THE NEW MERMAIDS

General Editor

BRIAN GIBBONS

Professor of English Literature, University of Münster

The Revenger's Tragedy

Edited by
BRIAN GIBBONS
Professor of English Literature
University of Münster

LONDON/A & C BLACK

NEW YORK/W W NORTON

Second Edition 1991
Reprinted 1992
Published by A & C Black (Publishers) Limited
35 Bedford Row, London WC1R 4JH
ISBN 0-7136-3232-1

© *1991 A & C Black (Publishers) Limited*

First published in this form 1967
by Ernest Benn Limited

© *1967 Ernest Benn Limited*

Published in the United States of America by
W W Norton & Company Inc.
500 Fifth Avenue, New York, NY 10110
ISBN 0-393-90060-6

Printed in England by Clays Ltd, St Ives plc

A CIP catalogue record for this book
is available from the British Library.

CONTENTS

SOURCES OF ILLUSTRATIONS

1   *Morte* from Ripa, *Iconologia*, 1600, by courtesy of the Folger Shakespeare Library, Washington

2 & 3   From Hans Holbein, 'The Dance of Death', 1538 facsimile edition of *Les simulachres et historiees faces de la mort* (New York, Dover, 1971)

4   From *The Kalender of Shepherds* (1592), reproduced in an article on *The Jew of Malta* by G. K. Hunter in *The Journal of the Warburg and Courtauld Institutes* (1964)

5 & 7   From Geoffrey Whitney, *A Choice of Emblemes* (Leyden, 1586)

6   From Geoffrey Whitney, *A Choice of Emblemes* (Leyden, 1586), by courtesy of the Folger Shakespeare Library, Washington

8   From *The Daunce and Song of Death*, a broadside ballad published in 1569, reproduced by W. Farnham in *The Medieval Heritage of Elizabethan Tragedy* (Oxford, 1936)

Once again for

LAURENCE JAGGER

PREFACE

This is a new edition, which presents a fresh commentary and a much amplified Introduction, with new sections on staging, the author, and the sources. The text has been re-edited and some of the lineation and a few textual readings have been changed, and the collation has been amplified.

BRIAN GIBBONS

ABBREVIATIONS

Editions of the play cited

Collins   *The Plays and Poems of Cyril Tourneur*, ed. J. Churton Collins, 2 vols (1878), vol. 1

Dodsley   *A Select Collection of Old English Plays*, published by Robert Dodsley, 12 vols (1744), vol. 4

Foakes   *The Revenger's Tragedy*, ed. R. A. Foakes (The Revels Plays, 1966)

Harrier   *Jacobean Drama*, ed. Richard C. Harrier, 2 vols (1963), vol. 2

Harrison   *The Revenger's Tragedy*, ed. G. B. Harrison (The Temple Dramatists, 1934)

Nicoll   *The Works of Cyril Tourneur*, ed. Allardyce Nicoll (1930)

Symonds   *The Best Plays of Webster and Tourneur*, ed. J. A. Symonds (1888)

Periodicals and reference works

Abbott   E. A. Abbott, *A Shakespearian Grammar* (1869)

E&S   *Essays and Studies*

ELR   *English Literary Renaissance*

NQ   *Notes and Queries*

OED   *A New English Dictionary*, ed. J. A. Murray, H. Bradley, W. A. Craigie, and C. T. Onions, 13 vols (1888–1933)

PQ   *Philological Quarterly*

SEL   *Studies in English Literature*

Tilley   M. P. Tilley, *A Dictionary of Proverbs in England in the Sixteenth and Seventeenth Centuries* (1950)

The Shakespeare quotations are taken from *The Riverside Shakespeare*, ed. G. Blakemore Evans (1974).

INTRODUCTION

THE AUTHOR

THE GROUNDS for attributing *The Revenger's Tragedy* to Cyril Tourneur are slight, and have been repeatedly disputed. The play was entered in the Stationers' Register on 7 October 1607, without an author being named: 'Twoo plaies th one called *the revengers tragedie* th other. *A trick to catche the old one.*'

The play was first attributed to Tourneur in 1656 by Edward Archer in a play-list, and Frances Kirkman followed suit in two play-lists in 1661 and 1671.

Recent academic opinion has seemed to want to attribute the play specifically to Thomas Middleton, on the basis of certain detailed common features of language and spelling in *The Revenger's Tragedy* and Middleton's works. There are no external grounds for Middleton's authorship.

The suggested atribution to Middleton had been made in the past, but it did not convince those who objected that the style and tone of Middleton's dramatic work, in the period before 1608, was too unlike that of *The Revenger's Tragedy*. The affinity of the play with the work of Marston, in terms of dramatic style, tone and subject-matter, seems very close, but does not provide sufficient grounds for attributing it to him, and it is clearly also close in style and temper to the later tragedies of Webster. A case has been made for linking the play's peculiarities of spelling, as well as its general features, to those of *The Atheist's Tragedy* (the one play Tourneur is firmly credited with). A general comparison of the two plays will recognise significant differences in style which scholars have sought to explain as the maturing of the author's art. There is not space here to go into detail about the many highly detailed discussions about the authorship of this play, and readers wishing to pursue the matter should consult the discussion in the edition by R. A. Foakes, and in the works by D. J. Lake and McD. P. Jackson in the list of Further Reading at the end of this Introduction.

In the first New Mermaid edition of *The Revenger's Tragedy* the undecided authorship problem was noted. It seemed, for reference sake, convenient to leave the attribution to Tourneur, as this was customary. Further reflection on *The Revenger's Tragedy*'s differences from *The Atheist's Tragedy*, on its difference from early Middleton, and on the absence of external evidence until 1656 of Tourneur's authorship, now persuades me to remove Tourneur's name.

The play is a minor masterpiece and is a unique response to a cultural moment, and a moment of the Jacobean theatre, with *Hamlet, The Phoenix, The Malcontent, Measure for Measure* and *King Lear* all recently performed – and *A Trick to Catch the Old One* newly written. The author of *The Revenger's Tragedy* had a distinctive intelligence; the mystery of his identity seems somehow consonant with the mood of his play, however accidental its cause; and there is always the possibility that he had a reason for remaining anonymous.

THE PLAY

Oh do not jest thy doom   (I. ii. 49)

Paradoxically, *The Revenger's Tragedy* does not lie in the main tradition of Elizabethan revenge tragedy; in fact it may be seen as the forerunner of a group of horror tragedies, breaking the pattern established two decades earlier in Kyd's *The Spanish Tragedy*.[1] The author certainly incorporates some essential elements of Kydian tragedy, but the play's vitality springs as much from other sources in Marston, in Henry Chettle's *Tragedy of Hoffman* (1603) and in Middleton's comedy. It may be tempting to over-emphasise the significance of the comic and farcical elements in the play, but Alfred Harbage[2] has reminded us that even Kyd employed comic methods with tragic materials and that intrigue is a characteristic element in Elizabethan tragedy. Nevertheless the use of comic method is plainly much more pervasive than Kyd's, or even Shakespeare's in *Titus Andronicus*.

F. T. Bowers acutely remarks that one suspects the author would have allowed Vindice to remain the hero had he not felt the lure of an unexpected ironic climax.[3] It is arguable that Vindice's fall comes about so abruptly, and with such flippancy, that it is in fact meant to be a joke – a bitter one.

We may be able to understand the play's art more readily by first considering the form of the play, and then examining the way in which the tragic theme is modified and shaped into this unique tragic burlesque. Formally, the play is related to three kinds of drama then popular: Senecan revenge tragedy, 'Comicall Satyre' in the style of Marston and intrigue comedy in the style of Middleton.

Firstly, Vindice desires to revenge his betrothed and also his dead father – though the latter only died of discontent. These are typical

[1] F. T. Bowers, *Elizabethan Revenge Tragedy 1587–1642*, new issue (1959), p. 138

[2] In *Essays . . . in Honour of Hardin Craig*, ed. R. Hosley (1962), p. 37

[3] Bowers, p. 134

M   O   R   T   E

1 The allegorical representation of Death

motives of the hero-revenger, and to them must be added his desire to purge the society of evil. Vindice, then, is a revenger of blood who believes his motives to be pure and so retains the characteristic heroic stance.

In devising his revenge, however, Vindice resembles the hero of Marston's *Malcontent*. Vindice devises an intrigue whereby he is lured by his enemy while disguised as a malcontent; operating in this and other disguises Vindice provokes discord among his enemies so that they plot against each other. In some sequences his disguise enables him to act as a detached, satirical and didactic commentator on the folly or evil of the other characters on stage. These self-sufficient sequences usually end with the exposure or punishment of such characters. *The Revenger's Tragedy*, like *The Malcontent*, has a form loose enough to allow such sequences to develop at length, as in I. iii, II. i or IV. ii.

2 The Dance of Death: Death in the costume of Folly seizes the Queen.

On the other hand, the play also contains several complex intrigues which are prosecuted with an urgency, a sinewy vigour in dialogue and a witty irony that insistently recall Middleton in *Michaelmas Term* or *A Trick to Catch the Old One* (1605 and 1605–6).[4]

These main formative influences are in some measure present – though not with assurance – in Henry Chettle's *Tragedy of Hoffman*, the play which, it seems, offered direct inspiration. For Chettle's hero is a villain who believes himself pure, who calls on heaven to show it supports him – and is answered. He is a resourceful deviser of intrigue who exults at his successes:

> Trickes, and devices! longings! well 'tis good:
> Ile swim to my desires, through seas of blood.[5]

He glories in the extreme cruelty of his revenge, and contrives a series of macabre, even gruesome scenes. An example of this is the murder of Otho, who is killed by a red-hot crown clamped to his head. As he dies Otho cries out

>   I feel an Aetna burne
> Within my braines, and all my body else
> Is like a hill of Ice ...
> My sinewes shrinke like leaves parcht with the sunne
> My blood dissolves, nerves and tendons faile.   (I.i)

When we turn to *The Revenger's Tragedy* itself we may be struck by the alternation between energetic, high-spirited action and brooding, slow-paced scenes of meditation on death, revenge and evil. This disturbing duality, reflected in the images of grinning skull and capering skeleton, derives partly from the medieval tradition of meditation on death, sin, and the contemptible foulness of the world, partly from a Classical and literary tradition of satire; the first profoundly personal in approach, the second essentially detached and witty.[6] There is a corresponding alternation of pace and mood in Vindice himself, now the high-spirited witty deviser of schemes, now the anguished and melancholy mourner, 'still sighing o'er Death's vizard'. Vindice's abrupt shifts, from his usual pose of witty superiority and immunity, to tragic involvement, indicate his change of *roles* – from satirist to revenger. There is a consequent change in dramatic method. This may be seen much more clearly by referring directly to the play, and I would like to illustrate from the

---

[4] *Works of Middleton*, ed. Rev. A. Dyce (1840)
[5] Henry Chettle, *The Tragedy of Hoffman*, ed. H. Jenkins (1961), V.ii
[6] For a fuller account of the distinction between Complaint and Satire see J. Peter, *Complaint and Satire in Early English Literature* (1956).

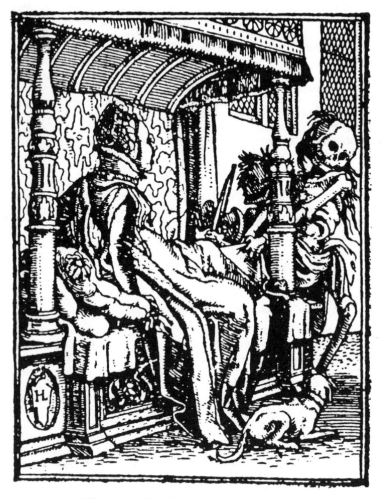

3 The Dance of Death: Death seizes the Duchess.

4 Souls damned for avarice

opening scenes. What is clear above all is that this dramatic method
subordinates character and incident to the author's main concern,
the presentation of a deeply ironic and disquieting view of human
nature. For such purposes a deliberately stylised and mannered
technique was fundamentally necessary.

The play opens with Vindice acting as a satiric Presenter of the
dumb show unwittingly furnished by the Duke, Duchess and
followers sweeping by in a blaze of torchlight. Vindice etches
their several characters in harsh terms, recalling the manner of

5 The emblem of God's all-seeing eye (Cf. Vindice's reference to 'that eternal eye/That sees through flesh and all'.)

Theophrastus and the verse satirists,[7] and his soliloquy illustrates clearly his habitual tendency to swing violently from gloom to gaiety. After a sustained bitter meditation on his lost love, made the more impressive by the visual effect – a black-clad figure gazing on a skull by dim torchlight – Vindice's gaiety erupts at the thought of his revenge, and his mind sharply visualises Revenge leading in the grinning, dancing skeletons to thrust his enemies into the cauldron of hell fire;[8] and, while this gleeful mood persists, his brother joins him.

The conversation between the brothers proceeds at the brisk pace to be expected from two witty and educated young nobles, and the spare, active verse drives their planning on:

VINDICE
  Brother I'll be that strange composed fellow.
HIPPOLITO
  And I'll prefer you brother.

[7] See, for example, Jonson's sketches of the characters prefixed to *Every Man Out Of His Humour* and John Donne's *Satires* I–IV.
[8] See plates 2 and 4.

VINDICE   Go to then,
  The small'st advantage fattens wrongèd men.
  It may point out Occasion;   (I. i. 95–8)

When they are joined by their mother and sister, the playful wit combat is replaced by a less open and assured tone; Vindice's hint of suspicion (never followed up, incidentally) about his father's death recalls Hamlet's:

VINDICE
       ... Surely I think he died
  Of discontent, the nobleman's consumption.
GRATIANA
  Most sure he did.
VINDICE   Did he? 'Lack, – you know all,

                                (I. i. 125–7)

It is characteristic that the playwright should reinforce the tone of uneasiness by leaving us to draw our own conclusions from the fact that Vindice speaks *aside* when conversing with his own mother. The playwright, no less than his hero, shapes incident with a tough, witty cynicism.

Indeed we have a sense of guiding, shaping purpose in the whole articulation of the scene. The rhythm is significant. It begins in meditative stillness; the entry of a character initiates the planning of an intrigue and provokes a display of satiric wit, and the entry of further characters brings mounting complexity and speed to the action and a prevalent tone of unsentimental, curbed cynicism and precarious, sardonic comedy. It is this rhythm which governs the play as a whole.

The next scene is primarily a self-sufficient demonstration of the evil of corrupt justice, and its form is highly reminiscent of Marston's work. The opening dialogue between the Duke and the Judge is wholly ironic, its dignified tone is deceptive, it has a seemingly unbroken patina. Only the implications of what is said betray the dramatist's concern to reveal how pervasive corruption mines all within, leaving the very vocabulary of justice and morality empty husks:

DUKE
                 ... Who dares now whisper
  That dares not then speak out ...
               ... our closest shame.
1 JUDGE
  Your Grace hath spoke like to your silver years
  Full of confirmed gravity; for what is it to have
  A flattering false insculption on a tomb   (I. ii. 8–13)

6 The emblem Occasion (Cf. I. i. 54 and note.)

The sententious condemnation merely intensifies the servility of
the Judge's flattery. In fact this ironic inversion of values is the key
to the whole situation in this scene. A prince is being tried for rape
by corrupt judges controlled by the rapist Duke, the Duke's other
sons plot to ensure a verdict of 'guilty', the Duchess pleads for
mercy on the grounds that the law should not have authority over
princes! The situation is unfolded with didactic clarity as a
sustained and thorough parody of order, and the judgement itself is
presented in the fastest comic quick-fire dialogue, reaching towards
a climax when a bathetic reversal snaps the tension and makes the
whole sequence ridiculous. The defendant Younger Son has treated
the trial as a farce from the beginning, of course, but the bastard
Spurio provides the most memorably comic line just at the point of
anti-climax:

7 The emblem of the serpent concealed by the innocent flower

1 JUDGE
  Let that offender –
DUCHESS   Live, and be in health.
1 JUDGE
  Be on a scaffold –
DUKE   Hold, hold, my lord.
SPURIO [*Aside*]   Pox on't,
  What makes my dad speak now?   (I. ii. 80–2)

The playwright's handling of this sequence is reminiscent of
Middleton in *Michaelmas Term* (1605), where the usurer Quomodo
and his assistants intrigue to enmesh the young prodigal Easy: they

persuade him to take a bond; he seems to assent, then draws back; the tension breaks with astringently comic bathos:

QUOMODO
    Well ... because I will not disgrace the gentleman, I'm content.
EASY
    No sir, now you would, you shall not.
QUOMODO
    [*Aside*] Cuds me, I'm undone! He's gone again.
SHORTYARD
    The net's broke.[9]

The trial scene concluded, the author changes the pace and mood: the Duchess draws Spurio the bastard aside to woo him, and though Spurio occasionally lightens the mood with a jest, the prevalence of heavily sensuous and sombre imagery and the arguments and pleas for incestuous love make a strong contrast with the trial scene. Though the verse is compellingly supple, rich in variation and deceptively flexible, its images insist on the pervasive and unrelieved evil of the lovers: the sharp danger of knives, the cold brilliance of jewels, their lovemaking is the strife of devils or the contracting of scabs. Nor does this parody of an idyll last more than a few moments; even as he kisses her, Spurio is planning an intrigue with her and, as she leaves, his mind is plotting busily. Thus again the intrigue comedy takes over from the scene of tragic portents.[10]

It is in the next scene (I. iii) that the promise of exuberant, gleeful action from Vindice, registered in his opening soliloquy, is fulfilled. His entry is vigorous indeed:

    What brother, am I far enough from myself?

and appropriately enough he invokes the spirit of impudence to give him aid; she does so, and Lord Lussurioso responds favourably to Vindice's greeting

    How dost sweet musk-cat? When shall we lie together?

Vindice offers an ominous yet striking jest, and the tone of slight uneasiness is marvellously caught by the brief catches in the dialogue's rhythm as Lussurioso is put off balance:

LUSSURIOSO
    What hast been – of what profession?

---

[9] *Works of Middleton*, vol. 1, p. 454
[10] Spurio recalls the bastard Edmund in *King Lear* in role, personality and involvement in sexual intrigues.

VINDICE
   A bone setter.
LUSSURIOSO
   A bone setter!
VINDICE
   A bawd my lord. One that sets bones together.   (42–5)

As the conversation proceeds, Vindice offers ostensible sympathy to Lussurioso and covert ridicule of him to the audience, and the comedy of the situation reaches its admirable climax in the passage where each of Vindice's responses is totally ambiguous, instinct with savage aggression while seemingly sympathetic. It is a typical example of Jacobean satiric comedy:

LUSSURIOSO
           . . . let thy heart to him
   Be as a virgin, close.
VINDICE   Oh my good lord.
LUSSURIOSO
   We may laugh at that simple age within him –
VINDICE
   Ha! Ha! Ha!   (138–41)

It is no less typical of the conventions of satiric comedy that Vindice should conclude the scene with a soliloquy of towering invective against the degeneracy and corruptness he has witnessed; the didactic function is as significant as the comic, though the latter has more vigour and assurance.

If this analysis has served to reveal how the dramatist varies the pace and mood in Act I, and how the alternate modes of tragedy and satiric comedy are articulated, it might be interesting to try and see the whole play in this perspective and hence learn something about its claims to the title of 'tragic burlesque'.

In Act I, as we have seen, satiric comedy is lively and even farcical; but though its subject-matter is unpleasant and disturbing, its action does not involve torture and murder. In the subsequent acts, however, the various intrigues initiated in Act I lead to increasingly horrific action before the eyes of the spectator. The mood and the tone of the dialogue in these scenes of torture and death are strikingly indecorous: it is, in fact, the mood and tone of comedy, and the profound, serious reflections on tragic themes, though voiced, are notably absent when death takes place. No character reflects on his own motives or state of grace; the dramatist plainly found more interest in Hamlet's murder of Polonius ('I'll lug the guts into the neighbour room') than in his inability to plot and execute revenge.

The first of such scenes is Lussurioso's attempted murder of the Duke (II. iii) and Vindice looks forward to it with a gleeful anticipation which recalls comic tricksters in Middleton, or Jonson's Mosca in *Volpone*; and when the attempted murder fails through Lussurioso's discovery, Vindice's reaction is wholly light-hearted. This attempt at murder fails, but the situation is based on a series of ironic reversals, and its conclusion ironically turns Lussurioso's attempt to revenge his father's honour into an attempt on his honour. But II. iii merely whets our appetite, and soon enough in III. iv the Younger Son is led off to execution by mistake: he cannot see his own death as anything but a sick joke:

> I thank you faith, good pretty wholesome counsel!
> I should look up to heaven as you said
> Whilst he behind me cozens me of my head!
> Ay, that's the trick. (68–71)

and his severed head serves as the focus of a farcical scene of mistaken identity (III. vi), with such absurd lines as

> Whose head's that, then?

and

> Villain I'll brain thee with it! (73, 77)

Act V begins with action and dialogue strongly reminiscent of Marlowe's *The Jew of Malta*; the stabbing of the corpse recalls Friar Jacomo's assault on the propped up corpse of Friar Barnadine – a double shock, mocking death and the Church. Marlowe's villain Ithamore intensifies the horror of that situation in gleeful tones:

> Ay, master, he's slain; look how his brains drop out on's nose.[11]

In *The Revenger's Tragedy* the mockery of death is effected with black humour:

VINDICE
> Sa, sa, sa, thump! [*He stabs the corpse*] There he lies!

LUSSURIOSO
> Nimbly done. [*Approaches the corpse*] Ha! Oh villains, murderers,
> 'Tis the old duke my father!

VINDICE [*Aside*]   That's a jest. (V. i. 60–2)

The last scenes of the play are indeed organised with an assured urbane skill; but there is more than a hint of comic method, comic form, and comic mood in the final scene itself. We might expect, knowing that the playwright borrowed the idea of the masque of

---

[11] *Plays* (World's Classics series, 1950), *The Jew of Malta* IV. 183

revengers from *The Malcontent*, that he would have carried over some of Marston's sombre seriousness also; but even here the farcical aspect remains dominant as a result of the author's duplication of masques. The first masque is, as it were, a *mask* concealing a rival group of revengers; when the original revengers arrive, their proposed victims are already dead, and this ironic reversal precipitates a wittier reversal as the murderers turn their swords upon each other. The second masque has concealed its threat of murder from its own actors, and this completed symmetry of pattern is tidy, though wrought out of carnage. Vindice himself jests with the dying Lussurioso, whispering torturing truth, turning his death rattle into a joke:

VINDICE
   Now thou'lt not prate on't, 'twas Vindice murdered thee!
LUSSURIOSO
   Oh.
VINDIVE   Murdered thy father!
LUSSURIOSO   Oh.
VINDICE   And I am he!
   Tell nobody. [LUSSURIOSO *dies*]   (V. iii. 80–2)

The valedictory words of Vindice have the lively, high-spirited tone of the successful comic trickster; it is impossible to take seriously the supposed tragic fall into sin of a character who leaves the stage with the words

                     we have enough –
I' faith we're well – our mother turned, our sister true
We die after a nest of dukes! Adieu.   (V. iii. 126–8)

Still, if it is true that the close of the play has comic vigour imparted to it by its hero and the resolution of complex interwoven plots, it is no less clear that the hero's blood revenge is achieved, and in as cruel a manner as could perhaps be imagined. It is the fact that Vindice's personal revenge is satisfied in III. v which gives scope for the working out of the various intrigues which either do not involve him at all or are additional to his main plan; but the scene of that revenge is of central importance in any discussion of the tragic aspects of the play, and it will perhaps be agreed that *The Revenger's Tragedy* has a tragic dimension.

   There are, as we saw in discussing Act I, several scenes in the earlier part of the play in which characters meditate on revenge, death and evil, though it is remarkable that their preoccupations are more generalised than we might expect – in fact they recall the reflections of medieval writers on sin and human frailty rather more readily than the self-centred thoughts of a tragic soliloquiser like

Hamlet. It is in these passages, however, that the playwright introduces a number of themes which find an intense and compelling focus in the long scene where Vindice's revenge on the Duke and on the evil he represents finds fulfilment. The image groups in the first three acts reverberate and gather meaning in a way comparable to those in *Hamlet*, and the tragic effect of III. v draws together the image patterns already established in preceding dialogue. It could be argued that the savagery of the actual murder and the harsh satiric cruelty of the vengeful brothers tend to reduce the full tragic effect rather than add to it; but the scene is masterly because the stagecraft, the actions and the iconographic effect (the groupings and movement as we *see* them) all contribute to its unity.

The preoccupations with death, sin and corruption which mark the meditative passages are expressed in images of food, land or flesh dissolving and putrefying. The speed and irreversibility of these processes is felt to be terrifying, and the metaphors of poison's corrosive action intensify this terror. To cuckold a husband is to lay acid on his brow:

> I'll kill him in his forehead, hate there feed – (I. ii. 107)

To ravish a woman is to consume her flesh: the Younger Son had 'long lust to eat' into Antonio's 'wearing' (clothing and flesh are equated as disguises for the skeleton in I. i) and finally succeeded

> And fed the ravenous vulture of his lust. (I. iv. 45)

The fusion of lust and disease is made in Spurio's cry

> Oh one incestuous kiss picks open hell (I. ii. 173)

and the idea of soft female flesh as a scab over putrefaction – a commonplace in medieval moral invective – is reiterated by Lussurioso:

> fairest women,
> Good only for their beauties, which washed off,
> No sin is uglier. (I. ii. 29–31)

Such images of disease corrupting beautiful female flesh are frequent not only in *Hamlet* but in Marston's comedies also, and the emblems and sculpture of the Renaissance period show a strong interest in the processes of decay and putrefaction.[12] Spurio's soliloquy in I. ii evokes the kinship of the appetites for food and for sexual pleasure:

---

[12] See Theodore Spencer, *Death and Elizabethan Tragedy* (1936) and plate 8.

> Faith if the truth were known I was begot
> After some gluttonous dinner – some stirring dish
> Was my first father; when deep healths went round
> And ladies cheeks were painted red with wine   (178–81)

but the diction is itself rotting with sweet sibilants –

> In such a whispering and withdrawing hour,
> When base male bawds kept sentinel at stair-head   (185–6)

and the epicurean dishes seem to be, though delicious, putrescent. This gives a strikingly sinister undertone to Vindice's subsequent ironic rhapsody on

> the stirring meats
> Ready to move out of the dishes
> That e'en now quicken when they're eaten   (II. i. 196–8)

and fuses the idea that sweetness and rottenness are synonymous, with the idea that disease lurks in beautiful flesh. Both beautiful, soft skinned women and epicurean dishes have in common the fact that when they dissolve they leave a stark and grimly durable frame of bones. Thus the metaphors and images drawn from skeleton and skull are linked thematically with those from food and diseased flesh.

These images have a sharp pictorial definition. In the case of those drawn from the Dance of Death there is a particular sharpness, due to the familiarity and frequency of illustrations of it at the time and, most important here, the fact that an actual skull is used in two key scenes of the play where it is the focus of the action and of the thematic imagery. Vindice's revenge on the Duke is to make him kiss the poisoned, painted mouth of a face once beautiful, now a naked skull. This act, which the audience watches, is the focus of the main themes of the imagery. It has a clear and exact ironic neatness, is wittily appropriate 'wild justice'[13] and is savagely cruel as a form of satiric ridicule and punishment.

Once in the summerhouse, the appointed scene for his revenge, Vindice delivers in superbly supple, hurrying, suddenly pausing rhythms his speech on the temptation of flesh and the suddenness of sin

> For the poor benefit of a bewitching minute   (III. v. 74)

and it is the discursive, vivid evocation of human weakness and infected spirit that creates the tragic dimension for Vindice's revenge, the climax of the play.

---

[13] Francis Bacon's definition in his essay *Of Revenge*, an illuminating introduction to the complicated Elizabethan attitude to the subject

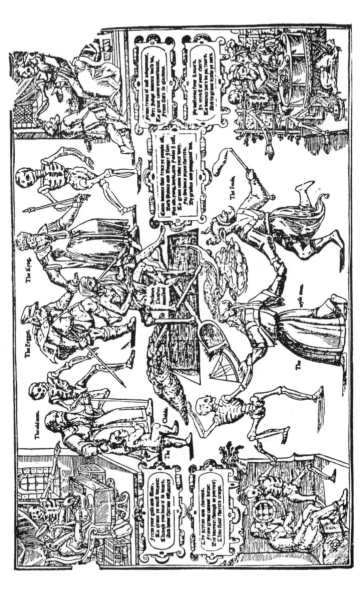

8 The Daunce and Song of Death: skeletons lead the Dance of Death to the tune of Sickness, Death's minstrel. The figures are the king, the beggar, the old man, the child, the wise man and the fool. Other skeletons invite the rich man, the judge, the prisoner and lovers to join the dance leading to the grave in the centre of the picture.

However Vindice is not a tragic hero comparable to Hamlet, Lear, Othello or Macbeth. Vindice has no inner conflict with temptation to evil, he suffers no indecision, no storm rages in his 'little world of man'. He neither doubts nor hesitates, he does not develop or decrease in stature, he achieves no deep self-knowledge. The tragic destruction which we sense in *The Revenger's Tragedy* is evoked in the context of society and mankind at large; and that context is the traditional concern of satiric, not tragic, art.

As I have tried to show, the revenge of Vindice draws the themes of the meditative passages into an intense and terrible focus. When Hippolito stamps on the dying Duke he reminds the audience of the pictures and sculptures and narratives showing the fate of damned souls, thrust down into the cauldron of hell by devils after the skeleton dancers have torn them away from their worldly pleasures. The intensity with which the playwright presents this terrifying experience, sustained by the superb, richly allusive and vivid imagery and the central significance of this theme to a Jacobean audience, gives us reason for describing the author as a tragic dramatist, though the uniqueness of his art lies elsewhere.

THE PLAY ON THE STAGE

The Development of Informed Interest

When I wrote the preceding part of this Introduction ('The Play') in 1966 for the 1967 edition, I had never seen the play performed.[14] I had seen the superb 1964 production of Marlowe's *The Jew of Malta* at the Aldwych Theatre, a production which was as invigorating for its influence on the staging of non-Shakespearean Elizabethan-Jacobean plays as was Peter Brook's production of *King Lear*, also of 1964, for the staging of Shakespeare.

This production of *The Jew of Malta* implicitly illustrated the parallels between Marlowe and Artaud, and was felt to display affinities between mid-sixteenth and mid-twentieth century power-politics. The performance of Eric Porter as Marlowe's Jew was essentially serious and made the character wholly convincing, even in the most farcically hilarious moments. The political-cultural turmoil he found himself in seemed consonant with the recent history of the Mediterranean, for instance in Cyprus, French Algeria, Palestine and Israel. (Since then Beirut has to be added.) The vitality of non-naturalistic modes of theatre had been largely

---

[14] The first known professional stage revival since the early seventeenth century had been performed three months earlier, in July 1965, at Pitlochry (as I learned several years later).

absent from the earlier twentieth-century British theatre, but after the revolutionary impact in London in 1956 of Beckett and Osborne and the visiting Berliner Ensemble's performance of Brecht, the way was open for Elizabethan-Jacobean drama's full theatrical language to be rediscovered by major professional (not only amateur) stage productions. Academic criticism since the 1930s had explored the drama of Shakespeare's contemporaries and provided theoretical underpinning and detailed commentary on many of the plays *as scripts for performance*, not merely for reading in the study. Scholars and critics, following the pioneering work of, for example M.C. Bradbrook and William Empson,[15] shared the aim of revaluing kinds of theatre in which moral psychology is not the primary concern, and which consequently had been previously considered of interest only to literary historians, antiquarians or cultural anthropologists, but too crude to be worth study as art, let alone worthy of professional stage performance. (This attitude extended to some of Shakespeare's plays as well, between the Restoration and the end of the nineteenth century.)

Changing attitudes to mixed-genre kinds of drama seem to have consolidated by the end of the 1950s in Britain, and a landmark in this evolution of taste was the appearance of J. L. Styan's book *The Dark Comedy* in 1962; this critical study of modern mixed-genre kinds of drama coincided with but also indirectly influenced a generally renewed appreciation of Elizabethan-Jacobean plays. Of course the Elizabethan-Jacobean outspokenness about political iniquity and the terrors of absolutist rule, with accompanying mental disorders of paranoia and psychopathic cruelty, and perverse sensual excesses, had seemed to nineteenth-century educated British readers to be rather vaguely related to their own social or political conditions, though immensely exciting in themselves.

In the first Mermaid edition of *The Revenger's Tragedy*[16] John Addington Symonds introduces Elizabethan revenge tragedy in terms which might have appealed to Byron – 'a romantic story of crime and suffering, a violent oppressor ... and suicides to end the action' – and his main interest is in the evocation of moral corruption and perverse eroticism: 'Vindice emerges from the tainted crew [of the court] with a kind of blasted splendour. They are curling and engendering, a brood of flat-headed asps, in the slime of their filthy appetites and gross ambitions ... The social corruption which has transformed them into reptiles, has made him

---

[15] See M. C. Bradbrook, *Themes and Conventions of Elizabethan Tragedy* (1935) and Empson's influential essay on double plots in *Some Versions of Pastoral* (1935).
[16] J. A. Symonds, ed. *The Best Plays of Webster and Tourneur* (1888)

a fiend incarnate' (p. xiv); to Symonds, Vindice is like Lucifer, like Cain, a satanic hero. Though Renaissance history might be read, its state cruelty was likely to be considered a thing of the past. A confidence in a general progress towards the rights of man and the rule of law, and social taboos surrounding sexuality and mental instability, typify the attitude of the educated middle class in the later Victorian period, when these plays began to be republished in the original Mermaid series.

The Victorian Robert Browning's poem 'My Last Duchess', a fictional dramatic monologue by an Italian Renaissance duke, in blank verse, reveals an informed understanding of the interplay of despotism and private psychological disorder, and one may also think it reminiscent of Elizabethan-Jacobean plays in its emphasis on the exoticism of Italy, where – it is evidently axiomatic – luxury and exquisite aestheticism are associated with sexual sadism and mortal sin. In his choice of an Italian setting Browning perhaps had in mind the middle-class prejudice and prudishness, and political complacency, of his English Victorian readers, who might find his study in sadism more palatable in an alien place, Italy, and a distant historical setting, than in (say) the Kensington of their own time.

This ambivalence about Italian culture is certainly a conscious concern of the best Elizabethan-Jacobean dramatists, but they choose Italian dukedoms as a location for their dramatic narratives for another reason too – because censorship forbade them from direct treatment of current English political issues, in their own country, on the Elizabethan stage. A knowledge of English history in the reigns of Elizabeth I and James I, or of European history merely since the 1930s, must rule out the idea that the subject-matter of this play is fantasy.

It is also certainly true that the theatrical mode partly determines the significance of its subject-matter, so that it is essential to have some understanding of the theatre as a playing space, and the conventions of characterisation, narrative and staging, which were common to the dramatists of the Elizabethan-Jacobean age. *The Revenger's Tragedy* is a play designed for practical performance in a theatre such as Shakespeare's Globe, and this is worth consideration before going on to notice some features of recent interpretations in the theatre of today.

The Play in the Jacobean Globe Theatre

The Revenger's Tragedy is a play much concerned with contemporary fashions – the silk and silver worn at court, the smart attitudes and witty indecencies of fashionable conversation, the modish indulgence in adultery and homosexuality, the taste for feasts, revels by night, and extravagant masques, above all the ruthless intrigues for promotion and consequent political and social prestige.

From the play's opening scene language and stage action give prominence to how characters are dressed and how they look; the original audience at the Globe Theatre were evidently treated to a parade of high contemporary fashion. (Drawings and paintings of the period show that English court fashions closely resembled those of Italy at this time when extravagant ostentation was at a peak.) It is worth recalling that at this period sumptuary laws restricted and prescribed what people of various social ranks might wear. The gorgeous costumes also constituted a sign-system of ranks, making the differences between nobility, gentry and servants ostentatious. Costume for noble women in the Jacobean court, especially masque costume, emphasised the forehead and left the breasts to a great degree exposed; both men and women wore jewellery, rich fabrics and high-heeled shoes.

This spectacular emphasis on costume, jewels and the body would have been enhanced by the requirement in a number of scenes in the play for torchlight, which may indeed have lived up to the hyperbolic remark that 'torchlight made an artificial noon'. At the Globe spectators would have attended performances in the afternoon, some of them standing out in the open in the unroofed yard, some sitting in the surrounding galleries. They faced the roofed wooden stage (as depicted on the cover of the present volume), and behind it there was a permanent wooden facade, probably decorated with carving or other ornamentation (which was used in the Elizabethan period equally for both internal and external wall surfaces). The new Swan Theatre at Stratford-on-Avon shows that a wooden stage and facade can as easily be accepted as representing a wooden Elizabethan interior as a city street. This essentially neutral but adaptable wooden setting would also be transformed by the imagination of spectators into presence-chamber, dungeon, palace great hall, bedchamber, or whatever the particular dialogue might indicate. Performances indoors, whether at court or at the Blackfriars Theatre (acquired by the King's Men in 1608), used artificial lighting but otherwise had a similar kind of non-representational playing-space.

Precisely because it was non-representational, such a playing-space was highly versatile and permitted a rapid transition from scene to scene, something which this play certainly requires. The space was also large enough for the staging of elaborate ceremonial, processions, tournaments, dances, masques, crowd-scenes and fighting; the rear facade had doors at either side, a central opening, and an upper acting area, and there were traps in the stage floor and the roof. The Swan Theatre at Stratford is a revelation in demonstrating what great versatility in staging is possible with the deceptively simple Elizabethan resources of wooden structure, ropes and pulleys, traps and ladders, a variety of entrances and exits (including through the spectators) and genuine, working properties. *The Revenger's Tragedy* makes only limited use of the Globe Theatre's range of special effects; it makes no use of the trap-door as in *Hamlet* or *Titus Andronicus*, or of the upper stage as in *The Spanish Tragedy*, or of any of the large stage properties which were available.

This economy in staging technique serves to intensify the focus on the characters, and the relationship between actor and spectator in the Globe Theatre was close, direct and lively. The play is full of colourful main-stage activity, with splendid ceremony and processions, dance and music, night scenes, corpses propped up in life-like attitudes, death by poisonous kissing or stabbing with cold steel, and scenes of erotic seduction or cruel interrogation. Since the dramatist concentrates all the emphasis on the human bodies of his actors, such economy is also a means to the making of exceptionally powerful effects, given the close and intimate relationship between actor and spectator in Elizabethan theatres. Thus the dramatist concentrates on the human bodies of his actors for his major visual effects, indicating carefully (often by implicit stage directions in the dialogue) how they are to look and position themselves. The play begins with Vindice watching a procession of the chief court characters, and it ends with the killing of these same characters as they in turn watch a masque danced in front of them. The emphasis on the human body of the actor is further stressed by the frequent requirement for disguising, whether it be Vindice with his changes of clothes and voice, or the 'bony lady', the lipstick-bedaubed skull of his mistress, which, dressed in a noblewoman's gown (and presumably a wig), serves to lure the Duke to an agonising death.

Thus in the play-world, clothes and paint, false voices and contrived manners offer success to those adept at self-fashioning,[17] but leave everyone vulnerable to deceptive surface appearances. Even Vindice, finally, is deceived by the appearance of benignity in the new duke, Antonio. This reflects the real English court of the time, where appearances counted for so much and leading courtiers amassed huge debts in the extravagant atmosphere.

It is consistent with the play's general emphasis on voracious appetite triumphing over basic Christian values that the threat of eternal judgement should be repeatedly invoked in *The Revenger's Tragedy*. It is invoked, furthermore, in terms of simple stage

---

[17] See Stephen Greenblatt, *Renaissance Self-Fashioning* (1980).

conventions, ominous thunder and the blazing star. No doubt this is partly due to the influence of the earlier Morality tradition, as L. G. Salingar pointed out,[18] but it also evidently was prompted by the very recent performance at the Globe of *King Lear*. In that play the king calls to the gods for thunder and lightning, the onset of apocalypse, as he goes mad, and indeed during the episodes of the storm the play seems also to enter a supernatural dimension. Lear's horrified vision of lust, greed and envy has hallucinatory vividness. At the same time Lear's mental derangement seems in many ways natural, like the storm itself: the status of the supernatural remains equivocal, however powerful its recall of Morality dramatic precedent or older superstition.

The Revenger's Tragedy, it could be said, revisits the sensually corrupt court of *The Malcontent* or *Hamlet* but in the new, apocalyptic terms of *King Lear*. The play yields to despair though finding distraction – as *King Lear* does not – in wit, mockery or protest. It is significant that it is a sub-plot of *King Lear* (concerning Edgar and Edmund) which is borrowed for *The Revenger's Tragedy's* plot, although it is the vision of King Lear himself which gives the play its dark compulsion and perhaps prompts its key stage images. 'You do me wrong to take me out of the grave', says the exhausted Lear: in *The Revenger's Tragedy* memorable and shocking use is made of a skull and of corpses, thus physically presenting on stage, and so intensifying, the obsessional fear of death and religious doubt. The play is fascinated by sensuous pleasure and physical cruelty, with the human body as at once a sensitive source of pleasure and an instrument to give and receive agony. In *The Revenger's Tragedy*, perhaps by deliberate choice, the question of apocalypse is turned aside so that the audience should be confronted with the ironies of power politics in the here and now. For that, bitter farce seems the appropriate mode.

Productions since 1965

It is easy to forget that most Elizabethan-Jacobean plays were performed, whatever their historical or geographical setting, in modern – that is, Elizabethan-Jacobean – dress. In the case of *The Revenger's Tragedy* the setting is a present-day, 1607, Italian dukedom. The dress of rich Jacobean courtiers was in fact similar to that of their Italian equivalents, and Italian style in luxury was much in vogue in England. This allowed the play's satire an equivocal status – it referred to England but its ostensible subject was foreign.

[18] '*The Revenger's Tragedy* and the Morality Tradition', *Scrutiny*, 1938

A modern production that sets the play in some different place and time should aim at reproducing the play's original satiric concern with current fashion. The idea of giving the play a non-Jacobean setting is not necessarily out of the question, so long as these provisos are borne in mind. There have been successful examples in Shakespearean production and with other plays of this period of settings in other places or periods – Ford's *'Tis Pity She's a Whore*, for example, made interesting sense when set in early nineteenth-century Italy.

Far more important than these considerations is the fact that great changes in culture separate the present day in Britain from the time of James I, particularly in the private and public importance of Christianity, in the nation's social structure, political assumptions and security systems, in the place of women, and in the knowledge of other cultures and races. The people who act plays today and the people who make up the audiences are in certain ways significantly different from the subjects of James I. Precisely because the play is in some ways remote, it may make us more aware, through contrast, of features of our own time and culture. It was *The Revenger's Tragedy*'s exploitation of 'black comedy' which seized the attention of reviewers who saw amateur productions in 1964 at Oxford and in 1965 at Cambridge,[19] for 'black comedy' was now of dominant interest in intellectual and theatrical fashion (Joe Orton's farce *Loot* is a period example). Black comedy was a strong ingredient in the 1964 Royal Shakespeare Company's concern with 'Theatre of Cruelty', including the *Marat/Sade*, *King Lear* and *The Jew of Malta*.

Thus the director of the 1966 production of *The Revenger's Tragedy* for the Royal Shakespeare Company, Trevor Nunn, explained 'It seemed to me a play that was extraordinarily about aspects of our own world . . . where the relationship between sex, violence and money was becoming increasingly popular, and expressed through all sorts of things – spy novels – James Bond. The "good life" – the life of extraordinary opulence and comfort – was connected with something fundamentally immoral . . . what fascinated me about [Vindice] was that he was totally schizophrenic; a completely modern study'.[20] Today's theatrical interpretations of Jacobean plays will – if they are to have truth and vitality of performance – express something of their own time and the

[19] Noted by Stanley Wells, '*The Revenger's Tragedy* Revived', in *The Elizabethan Theatre VI* (1975). I am indebted to this article for the details it records of the Trevor Nunn production. I myself saw the play at Stratford, from the cheapest and most remote part of the house, where it nevertheless made a lively impression.

[20] David Addenbrooke, *The Royal Shakespeare Company* (1974), pp. 137–8, cited by Wells, p. 106

concerns of their own audiences; a purely 'archaeological' interpretation can have little power over a live audience, and it should be stressed that when first performed *The Revenger's Tragedy* addressed urgent issues of its time in avant-garde style. A comparable sense of directness and anxiety must be created in performance today if the play is to be brought alive.

If one compares the production by Nunn at the Royal Shakespeare Theatre in 1966 with that by Di Travis in 1987 at the Swan Theatre, this issue becomes clearer, while something of the play's recent theatrical life can be seen. The 1966 production utilised the very large main theatre at Stratford-on-Avon. It was also seen (at last, in 1969) at the large Aldwych Theatre in London. Both these playhouses had been originally built with proscenium-arch stages and a large auditorium, requiring an appropriate scale of performance and actors able to project it in so large a space. Because the play was new to the modern professional theatre it was assumed that it would lose money; it had a low budget and was played in the company's *Hamlet* set, and it was planned to have only eight performances.

The set was 'an open, black, shining "box", with two huge doors opening at the rear ... The basic material was black formica'.[21] A reviewer noted how hinged walls at the back of the set were used to create various shapes of acting area 'and a tall canopy throne ... floats down the centre of the stage for the Duke'.[22] A huge silver circle on the black floor was used to formalise groupings. The Duke at its centre was costumed in glittering silver; 'as one moved further from this centre, the costumes on stage became less silver and more black'.[23] The costume designs were basically dresses and stomachers for the women and breeches for the men, with additions to indicate higher rank or status. The basic colour was silver over black. The reviewer for *The Times* commented that the courtiers were dressed uniformly in silver and black as if to stress that Vindice 'is fighting corporate evil rather than isolated individuals';[24] the effect was reinforced by large-scale choreography of precise, meaningful movement and grouping, and the invention, aided by portable properties, of precise contexts for many scenes – in short, it was essentially faithful to the stagecraft of the Jacobean theatre.

The performance of the play itself was prefaced by an invented dumb-show. The courtiers 'surge forward from a deep black box, brandishing masks and torches: as they swish in patterns about the

[21] Addenbrooke, p. 130
[22] B. A. Young, *The Financial Times*, 6 October 1966, cited by Wells, p. 115
[23] Addenbrooke, p. 145
[24] Review in *The Times*, 6 October 1966

stage, like brilliants juggled on black velvet, we get a clue about who's being raped, who's in charge, who's paying court to whom'.[25] The mime showed Antonio's wife first being hemmed in by cloaked courtiers, then pushed down in the centre of the circle, her head facing down-stage. Junior leapt on top of her, and the courtiers hid them from view, rhythmically raising and flapping their cloaks 'as vultures' wings'.[26] The woman screamed and the group dispersed.

The precise scenic contexts may be illustrated by some examples. The scene where Vindice, in disguise, first meets Lussurioso was set in a fencing school – indicated by two lines of fencers, all masked, when the scene opened – and Vindice and Lussurioso fought one bout in public, and then another alone. Finally Vindice was disarmed, and both took off their fencing-masks; then, swearing to be true, Vindice kissed Lussurioso's sword.

'The next scene, between Vindice and Castiza, was played with a number of dressmaker's dummies on stage, as if to suggest a profession for Castiza. When Vindice had to show Gratiana gold, he took material from a dummy, spread it on the ground, and put jewels on it. Gratiana went on her knees to them.

'Act II, scene ii, which is mostly a conversation between Vindice and Lussurioso, showed Lussurioso practically naked, lying on a slab and being oiled and stroked by a plump masseur who looked like a dumb eunuch'.[27]

In each of these instances a precise social context and activity wittily substantiated the spoken dialogue and helped the characters interrelate in comprehensible ways. Their physical gestures and actions, their dress and appearance, had an immediate credibility and also came to have metaphoric significance. What was performed on stage clarified the public and private politics, enhanced certain images in the text, and enriched characterisation; at the same time certain modern preoccupations evidently influenced the whole treatment of the play.

The treatment of spectacle of a grander kind was no less interesting. Act III, scene v featured a tomb property on which Vindice seated the 'bony lady', a 'scarecrow figure dressed in a robe and topped by the skull'. The promptbook calls for the Duke to climb on top of this figure on the tomb and kiss it. Then Vindice and Hippolito pushed the Duke down onto it and held him, with daggers at his heart and tongue, forcing him to watch his wife making love with Spurio (this she did in a kind of erotic dance with torches). The Duke was stabbed under cover of loud music from a

[25] D. A. N. Jones, 1966, cited by Wells, p. 116
[26] *The Listener*, 4 December 1969
[27] Wells, p. 117

banquet. He showed the audience his butchered face as he died. Act IV, scene ii, Lussurioso's hiring of Vindice in propria persona, was played against a background of victims being tortured on racks, Lussurioso enjoying their agony as he worked the levers.[28]

The scene of Lussurioso's investiture was a visually strong set-piece. 'The walls at the back of the set opened to admit guards with torches, and a procession in five ranks, led by Lussurioso, advanced . . . in slow and ritualistic fashion. The empty throne followed them. The members of each rank of the procession turned their backs to the audience, the stiff fabric of their robes swishing sinisterly with each obscene thrusting forth of their bodies'.[29] Lussurioso mounted the throne, received their hypocritical obeisance and then raised his arm in a totalitarian salute which they returned. The blazing star was not represented (nor had thunder been, earlier), but it was imagined as if in the audience, and Lussurioso collapsed on seeing it.

For the final dance of revengers, skull-masks were worn, and the masquers danced 'metronomically to the insistent rhythm of an off-stage drum. They bore swords which they clashed together in the dance, like morris-dancers' (so visually recalling the dance of the Duchess with Spurio which used torches in a similar way). They leapt on the table to kill their victims, who also wore skull-masks.

Harold Hobson, offering a minority reaction, did not think the play an exposure of a corrupt society but rather 'an encyclopaedia of moral obscenities', otherwise dealing 'only in elementary misdemeanours'.[30] He did not enjoy the burlesque element. Ian Richardson in the role of Vindice was the source of much of the burlesque comedy in this production, his changes of mood very sudden, manic energy replaced abruptly by 'a frightened, serious silence'.[31] A foil was provided by the extreme corruption and foppishness of Alan Howard's Lussurioso. A slapstick element was reinforced by the grotesque farcical portrayals of Ambitioso, who was tall, high-heeled, mincing, and Supervacuo, who was squat and dumpy. Above all the pervasive dark influence of the black set and black-and-silver costumes remained strong, however much laughter the wit and burlesque generated.

An appropriate contrast is provided by the 1987 production, performed in a much smaller theatre, the Swan, at Stratford, and then later on tour in various provincial playhouses. The decision was made to present both *The Jew of Malta* and *The Revenger's*

---

[28] Summarised from Wells, pp. 118–19

[29] Ibid., pp. 120–1

[30] *The Sunday Times*, 9 October 1966

[31] Gareth Lloyd-Evans, *The Stratford-on-Avon Herald*, 13 October 1966

Tragedy in 1987, in the same playhouse and in the same season. This suggests that parallels were sensed once again (as they had been in the mid-sixties) with the Jacobean age. The actor cast as Vindice was Anthony Sher, who also played the Jew in *The Jew of Malta* in the same house. At the beginning of the 1980s Sher had won acclaim with the company for a flamboyant interpretation of the crookback, murderous machiavel, Richard III. Sher had had success in roles which embodied something of the quick-fire, amoral new mood of the mid 1980s, with the new wave of political authoritarianism and of ostentatious capitalist prosperity in the City. A certain ambivalence towards the new wealth was apparent in an accompanying new vogue for cruel farce and satire in the 1980s (seen at its extreme in the caricature-puppets of television's *Spitting Image*). This ambivalence was apparent also in the West End success which greeted the satiric city comedy by Caryl Churchill, *Serious Money*.

The Swan production of *The Revenger's Tragedy* by Di Trevis in 1987 gave an impression of small scale. This was not so much due to the fact that fewer actors took part but rather to a decision to confine it to a restricted space, dominated by a single set presenting an oblique composition of decay. Tattered and faded drapes, of haphazard lengths, hung above. A sloping ramp, buried in a heap of rubble, was stage centre, and next to it a concealed hole covered by removable planks. An atmosphere of gloom was enhanced by elaborate lighting effects and dry ice.

This set gave only a vague impression of a time or place; only the occasional figure of a starving, ragged beggar emerging from or scurrying back to its shelter transformed it into a recognisable contemporary image of London destitution. This visual allusion was not developed or integrated into the production. The set was a dominant surreal image to which the costumes were keyed in colour and style, seeming decayed and deliberately vague in their suggestion of elaborate seventeenth-century court fashions. The general impression was a fantasy of decay, although when the sloping ramp was treated matter-of-factly as a table, the effect recalled the disquieting early German expressionist cinema, as in *The Cabinet of Dr Caligari*.

The tone was set by the physically hard vigour of Sher as Vindice and Nicholas Farrell, who played Lussurioso. They gave intelligent, external interpretations. Vindice was seen using makeup and red colouring powder on his hair to effect his disguise, and dared to caress Lussurioso with seemingly practised erotic art at their first meeting. It was characteristic of this production that specific contexts were not created for episodes such as this.

Most of the indications in the text and stage directions for spectacle were treated with restraint. A good deal of business was invented involving the obscure hole, but at the performance I saw, its significance was not really clear. Certainly the staging deliberately ignored the fuller staging resources of the Swan. Processions, ceremonies, and banquet murders have been impressively staged there in productions such as *Titus Andronicus*. Instead, this production took a deliberate line in blurring a sense of the play's location in time or place, and this enabled it to stress disorientation, anxiety and emptiness as key elements of the play-world. Power gave no protection, wealth was tawdry, luxury abruptly turned into deprivation, the aggressive physicality barred other ways of feeling. Toughness was the key, making the production a fable inclining to pitilessness, although this tended to foreclose a still unextinguished sense of the variety of experience, which a reading of the text affords.

These two productions contrast significantly in their treatment of the play, while both show that any modern staging of a Renaissance play will reflect aspects of its own time. Trevor Nunn's production was, for all its changes and additions to the text, remarkably faithful to the implicit and explicit directions for staging. It is ironic that his 1966 production, though played in playhouses markedly different from the Globe, was more sensitive to the playwright's full theatrical language than the Swan production.

SOURCES

Discussion of a play's sources is a complex matter, since dramatic construction involves a visual, non-verbal sign-system as well as a verbal one. In a play there are characters and plots, which may derive from other written sources, but there are also silent stage images which may derive from preceding plays. Such stage images might be of the particular character-type (the black-clad melancholic, the beautiful heroine, the fool) or larger groupings on stage, or images made significant through an actor's physical attitude, or through memorable and telling gesture, also perhaps involving the use of stage properties (the Hamlet-like detached observer with the skull, in the play's first scene, is an obvious instance of this).

The dramatists of the early Jacobean period in London habitually worked in conventions of genre, characterisation and plot, and relied on shared, familiar techniques of scenic construction, since the stages on which the plays were performed were few in number and sufficiently similar for the same play to be performed in different playhouses with relatively little modification. The plays were in any case readily adaptable, and the chief factor of concern, when a play was revived, was likely to be the number of actors available to perform it, not any specifically technical problems of staging. In fact *The Revenger's Tragedy* makes only modest demands of staging resources: there is no requirement of an upper stage, and the requirement of a bed to be put forth was a conventional one, with precedents in early Shakespeare plays, such as *II Henry VI* or *Romeo & Juliet*.

The play's title announces its kinship with an extremely popular and important dramatic genre – revenge tragedy – which featured some of the most famous plays of the period including (in reverse chronological order) *Hamlet, Titus Andronicus* and *The Spanish Tragedy*, and it has allusions to a number of other more recent plays, including *King Lear* (1605) and *Measure for Measure* (1604) and Marston's *The Malcontent* (1603–4). These allusions are usually meant to be recognised, and their self-consciousness probably appealed to audiences who had themselves recently seen the plays performed in the same playhouse, the Globe, by the same company, the King's Men (called on the title-page the King's Majesties Servants). At the same time these echoes of earlier plays, both verbal and visual, also indicate the dramatist's concern to work within the parameters of established dramatic conventions. The dramatic techniques had proven worth; audiences had responded to them. The effect of allusions is complex: they signal parallels with the tone, mode and plot-situation of an earlier work, but in calling attention to the parallel they also make a spectator aware of the specific new twists and differences in the present context. While these parallels in *The Revenger's Tragedy* to earlier plays are substantial in both style and plot, there is nevertheless also a non-literary, historical basis to the story the play dramatises. This was pointed out by N. W. Bawcutt in his article '*The Revenger's Tragedy* and the Medici Family' (*NQ* 202, 1957). J. W. Lever in his book *The Tragedy of State* (1971) says that the details of this historical episode in the Medici family, the assassination of Alessandro de' Medici in 1537, which are featured in *The Revenger's Tragedy*, could not have been found in the suggested literary source, Marguerite de Navarre's *Heptameron*, novel 12 of day 2, printed in Painter's *Palace of Pleasure* (1567). Lever notes that a significant number of detailed parallels between the action of the play and the historical events indicate that the dramatist must have had 'more direct access to the historical facts' than the *Heptameron* provides. Lever refers to the account of Alessandro de' Medici's assassination in Benedetto Varchi's *Storia Fiorentina*, lib xv.

A minor literary source has been suggested for the episode in Act II, scene iii where Lussurioso, with drawn sword, thinks to surprise the Duchess in bed with Spurio but finds her with the Duke instead.

This has been suggested as deriving from Book I of Heliodorus, *Aethiopia*, translated by Thomas Underdowne (1587). However, the episode could as well have been invented by the dramatist under the influence of Italianate tragi-comedy or (more simply still) *Hamlet*.

This instance well illustrates the difficulty of ascertaining sources for a play written at a period of intense dramatic activity in the restricted number of playhouses in London, especially when the playwright in question was highly susceptible to the imaginative stimulus of such powerful and distinctive fellow playwrights as Marston, Shakespeare and Middleton, assuming that Middleton is not the play's author. J. W. Lever forcefully argues for the direct influence of contemporary events and social circumstances on the dramatist's imagination, and notes how the details of court life and luxurious expenditure are no exaggeration, being amply documented ˙ historical fact. He illustrates this by referring, with precision, to contemporary conditions described in, for example, G. P. V. Akrigg, *Jacobean Pageant* (1962). More recent historical and literary studies multiply illustrations of this aspect of *The Revenger's Tragedy*.

THE TEXT

The play was first printed in 1607 by George Eld; in the following year sheets of this edition were made up and issued under a variant title-page. My copy-text for the present edition has been the copy of the second issue (British Museum 644 c 80), and with it I have collated the 1607 issue (C 34 e 11) also in the BM. I have also collated editions by Allardyce Nicoll and Richard Harrier and (for the 1990 new edition) that by R. A. Foakes. The presswork for the printing has been analysed by George Price (see *The Library*, vol XV). Price accounts for the high incidence of variants in signature H. More recently McD. P. Jackson in his Introduction to a facsimile of Q1, 1983, listed the stints of two compositors in setting the text. These compositors worked for the printer Eld in 1607–8 on a number of plays by several dramatists; Jackson believes that as they followed known orthographical preferences when setting the plays of other dramatists, he can be confident that the 'linguistic pattern of *The Revenger's Tragedy* is not a product of the printing house'.

Q has many detailed stage directions, one or two for actions not indicated by the dialogue: e.g. III.v.155, IV.ii.43. Speech prefixes are generally clear and specific except for, e.g., minor Nobles in Act V. Some exits and entrances are not marked.

In producing a modernised critical edition I have regularised,

amplified or added stage directions and speech headings where
necessary. I have rearranged the copy-text's lineation in places
where the compositors seem to have been unable to distinguish
verse from prose. Some of these places remain exceptionally
difficult problems of lineation, since in certain speeches transition
from verse to prose and back again seems to take place. Editors
have arranged certain verse passages in a variety of lineation and
have disagreed about the verse/prose status of several other
passages. The problem is associated with the more supple rhythms
of dramatic blank verse in early Jacobean drama (a somewhat
parallel lineation problem is seen in Shakespeare's *Measure for
Measure*, 1604). In the present new edition a consistent approach to
lineation has been applied, and details are recorded in the notes on
collation at the foot of each page. Substantive changes to the copy-
text are recorded in these notes, although modernised spelling,
expanded abbreviations and non-substantive corrections have been
silently made.

FURTHER READING

Allardyce Nicoll, *The Works of Cyril Tourneur* (1929, new issue 1963)

M. C. Bradbrook, *Themes and Conventions of Elizabethan Tragedy* (1935)

L. G. Salingar, '*The Revenger's Tragedy* and the Morality Tradition', *Scrutiny*, 1938 (repr. in Salingar, *Dramatic Form in Shakespeare and the Jacobeans*, 1986)

Hardin Craig, 'The Shackling of Accidents', *PQ*, 19 (1940), repr. in R. J. Kaufmann, ed., *Elizabethan Drama, Modern Essays in Criticism* (1961)

F. T. Bowers, *Elizabethan Revenge Tragedy 1587–1642* (new issues, 1959)

N. W. Bawcutt, '*The Revenger's Tragedy* and the Medici Family', *NQ*, 202, 1957

Alvin Kernan, *The Cankered Muse* (1959)

Peter B. Murray, *A Study of Cyril Tourneur* (1964)

The Revenger's Tragedy, attributed to Cyril Tourneur, ed. R. A. Foakes (1966)

J. W. Lever, *The Tragedy of State* (1971)

Arthur C. Kirsch, *Jacobean Dramatic Perspectives* (1972)

R. A. Foakes, 'The Art of Cruelty: Hamlet and Vindice', *Shakespeare Survey 26*, 1973, pp. 21–32

David J. Lake, *The Canon of Thomas Middleton's Plays* (1975)

G. K. Hunter, 'Flat-caps and Blue-coats', *E&S*, 1980

Michael E. Mooney, 'This Luxurious Circle', *ELR*, 1983

The Revenger's Tragedy, attributed to Thomas Middleton, a facsimile introduced by McD. P. Jackson (1983)

Scott McMillin, 'Acting and Violence: *The Revenger's Tragedy* and its Departures from *Hamlet*', *SEL*, 1984

Charles R. Forker, *Skull Beneath the Skin, The Achievement of John Webster* (1986); see chapter 5, 'The Love-Death Nexus in English Renaissance Tragedy'

Dieter Mehl, 'Corruption, Retribution and Justice in *Measure for Measure* and *The Revenger's Tragedy*' in E. A. J. Honigmann, ed., *Shakespeare and his Contemporaries* (1986)

Leonard Tennenhouse, *Power on Display* (1986)

Charles R. Forker, '"A little more than kin and less than kind": incest, intimacy, narcissism and identity in Elizabethan and Stuart drama', *Medieval and Renaissance Drama in England*, 4, 1989, pp. 13–51

A. R. Braunmuller and Michael Hattaway, ed. *The Cambridge Companion to English Renaissance Drama* (Cambridge 1990), pp. 301–52

THE
REVENGERS
TRAGÆDIE.

As it hath beene sundry times Acted,
by the Kings Maiesties
Seruants.

Cy. Tourneur

AT LONDON
Printed by G. E l d, and are to be sold at his
house in Fleete-lane at the signe of the
Printers-Presse.
1 6 0 8.

[DRAMATIS PERSONAE

THE DUKE
LUSSURIOSO, *the Duke's son*
SPURIO, *a bastard of the Duke's*
AMBITIOSO, *the Duchess' eldest son*
SUPERVACUO, *the Duchess' second son*
YOUNGER SON *of the Duchess*
VINDICE, *a revenger, also called* PIATO *in disguise* ⎱ *brothers to*
HIPPOLITO, *also called* CARLO ⎰ *Castiza*
ANTONIO ⎱ *Nobles*
PIERO ⎰
DONDOLO
Nobles, Judges, Gentlemen, Officers, Keeper, Servants
THE DUCHESS
CASTIZA
GRATIANA, *mother of Castiza*]

Note on the names: Lussioroso = 'lecherous'; Spurio = 'a bastard'; Ambitioso = 'ambitious'; Supervacuo = 'superfluous, vain'; Vindice = 'a revenger of wrongs . . . and abuses, one that restoreth and setteth at libertie or out of danger'; Piato = 'flat, plated'; Dondolo = 'a gull, a fool' (these are the translations in Florio, *A Worlde of Wordes*, 1598); Castiza, from *casta*, 'chaste'; Gratiana, from *gratia*, 'grace'

THE REVENGER'S TRAGEDY

Act I, Scene i

Enter VINDICE; [*then*] *the* DUKE, DUCHESS, LUSSURIOSO *her son,*
SPURIO *the bastard, with a train, pass over the stage with
torchlight*

VINDICE
  Duke: royal lecher: go, grey haired Adultery,
  And thou his son, as impious steeped as he:
  And thou his bastard true-begot in evil:
  And thou his duchess that will do with devil:
  Four ex'lent characters! – Oh that marrowless age   5
  Would stuff the hollow bones with damned desires,
  And 'stead of heat kindle infernal fires
  Within the spendthrift veins of a dry duke,
  A parched and juiceless luxur. Oh God! one
  That has scarce blood enough to live upon,   10
  And he to riot it like a son and heir?
  Oh the thought of that
  Turns my abusèd heart-strings into fret.
  Thou sallow picture of my poisoned love,
  My study's ornament, thou shell of Death,   15
  Once the bright face of my betrothed lady,
  When life and beauty naturally filled out

---

4 *do* copulate
5–6 *marrowless . . bones* Vindice (as T. S. Eliot said of Webster) is much obsessed
  by death and sees the skull beneath the skin. The spectator sees a proud courtly
  procession but Vindice sees instead that age withers the body, the bone marrow
  no longer produces the healthy blood of youth. In place of fertile passion the
  frenzy of mortal sin goads the Duke, who ignores these warnings of approaching
  death and judgement.
7 *infernal fires* The damned suffer the fires of hell, and a burning sensation is a
  symptom of various venereal diseases.
8 *dry* withered and sterile
11 *like . . . heir* The prodigal son is a stock type in dramatic satire of city and court
  at this period; ambitious courtiers in fact spent huge sums to promote their
  interests at court. The new king, James, also indulged in lavish expenditure.
13 *fret* anger (and with a musical pun, as in *Hamlet* III. ii. 370–72: 'Call me what
  instrument you will, though you fret me you cannot play upon me')
14 Vindice addresses a skull, the 'sallow picture' of his poisoned love.

5

These ragged imperfections;
When two heaven-pointed diamonds were set
In those unsightly rings – then 'twas a face   20
So far beyond the artificial shine
Of any woman's bought complexion
That the uprightest man – if such there be,
That sin but seven times a day – broke custom
And made up eight with looking after her.   25
Oh she was able to ha' made a usurer's son
Melt all his patrimony in a kiss,
And what his father fifty years told
To have consumed, and yet his suit been cold:
But oh accursed palace!   30
Thee when thou wert apparelled in thy flesh,
The old duke poisoned,
Because thy purer part would not consent
Unto his palsey-lust; for old men lustful
Do show like young men angry-eager, violent,   35
Out-bid like their limited performances –
Oh 'ware an old man hot and vicious:
'Age as in gold, in lust is covetous'.
Vengeance, thou Murder's quit-rent, and whereby
Thou show'st thyself tenant to Tragedy,   40
Oh keep thy day, hour, minute, I beseech,
For those thou hast determined. Hum, who e'er knew
Murder unpaid? Faith, give Revenge her due,
She's kept touch hitherto – be merry, merry,
Advance thee, oh thou terror to fat folks   45

19–20 The diamond ring's durability is ironically contrasted to the eyes of his
   spiritually bright but tragically short-lived beloved. Vindice is imaginatively
   preoccupied with eyes and eye sockets; see I. iii. 8–10.
   unsightly (i) unseeing, (ii) ugly
22 *bought complexion* face made up with cosmetics
25 *after* at
27 *patrimony* property or estates inherited from ancestors
28 *told* counted up, amassed
29 *cold* unsuccessful
34–6 i.e., the lust of old men is like the violence of young men, limited in
   performance
35 *angry-eager* apparently a compound adjective
36 *out-bid* inadequate, out-bidden by others who are stronger
39 *quit-rent* rent paid by a tenant in lieu of service: hence, vengeance as murder's
   due
42 *determined* chosen, condemned
42–3 *Hum . . . unpaid?* alluding to the proverb 'Murder will out, murder cannot be
   hid' (See IV. ii. 206 below.)

To have their costly three-piled flesh worn off
As bare as this – for banquets, ease and laughter
Can make great men, as greatness goes by clay,
But wise men, little, are more great than they.

Enter [his] brother HIPPOLITO

HIPPOLITO
  Still sighing o'er Death's vizard?
VINDICE   Brother welcome,   50
  What comfort bring'st thou? How go things at Court?
HIPPOLITO
  In silk and silver brother: never braver.
VINDICE   Puh,
  Thou play'st upon my meaning, prithee say
  Has that bald madam, Opportunity,
  Yet thought upon's, speak, are we happy yet?   55
  Thy wrongs and mine are for one scabbard fit.
HIPPOLITO
  It may prove happiness?
VINDICE   What is't may prove?
  Give me to taste.
HIPPOLITO   Give me your hearing then.
  You know my place at Court.
VINDICE   Ay, the duke's chamber.
  But 'tis a marvel thou'rt not turned out yet!   60
HIPPOLITO
  Faith I have been shoved at, but 'twas still my hap
  To hold by the duchess' skirt, you guess at that –
  Whom such a coat keeps up can ne'er fall flat –
  But to the purpose.
  Last evening predecessor unto this,   65
  The duke's son warily enquired for me,
  Whose pleasure I attended: he began

---

46 *three-piled* finest velvet (having the thickest pile). Compare the clothing image
   of line 31 above.
48 *by clay* in terms merely of flesh
49 *little* of low rank. Foakes compares the proverb 'Wisdom is better than riches'
   (Tilley T 311).
51 *things* affairs. Hippolito's satiric answer makes 'things' become the dehumanised
   fops at Court who 'go' about dressed lavishly in silk and silver.
54 *Opportunity* Also known as Occasion (see plate 6 and lines 98–100 below).
   Occasion was depicted as a woman with a long forelock standing on a turning
   wheel, bearing a razor in her hand: her forelock had to be seized. She shared
   emblems of fickleness with Fortune (see *Henry V* III. vi for Fluellen's account
   of Fortune).

By policy to open and unhusk me
About the time and common rumour:
But I had so much wit to keep my thoughts   70
Up in their built houses, yet afforded him
An idle satisfaction without danger.
But the whole aim and scope of his intent
Ended in this: conjuring me in private
To seek some strange digested fellow forth   75
Of ill-contented nature, either disgraced
In former times, or by new grooms displaced
Since his step-mother's nuptials: such a blood,
A man that were for evil only good;
To give you the true word some base-coined pandar.   80

VINDICE

I reach you, for I know his heat is such,
Were there as many concubines as ladies
He would not be contained, he must fly out.
I wonder how ill-featured, vile proportioned
That one should be, if she were made for woman,   85
Whom at the insurrection of his lust
He would refuse for once: heart, I think none;
Next to a skull, though more unsound than one,
Each face he meets he strongly dotes upon.

HIPPOLITO

Brother y'ave truly spoke him!   90
He knows not you, but I'll swear you know him.

68-9 i.e., artfully to sound me out on recent events and what people are saying
about them

70-1 *keep ... houses* keep my real opinions to myself

72 *idle satisfaction* token answer

75 *strange digested* of unusual, odd or melancholic disposition. The malcontent is a
type in drama of the time (see Marston's play of 1603 called *The Malcontent*).
Melancholy was associated with madness as well as dark moods: it was believed
to be physiological, though it might also be triggered by frustrated ambition or
injustice.

78 *step-mother's nuptials* This is oddly specific, as if the dramatist meant to remind
spectators of *Hamlet* (although there it is a step-*father*, Claudius, who marries
the hero's mother, Gertrude).

80 *base-coined* The association of begetting children and coining money is
memorably expressed in *Measure for Measure* II. iv. 45-6, which may be in the
dramatist's memory here.

81 *reach* understand

84-7 i.e., there's no woman his lust would refuse, however ugly

88 *unsound* diseased, with pun as in *Measure for Measure* I. ii. 55-7: 'Nay, not (as
one would say) healthy; but so sound as things that are hollow. Thy bones are
hollow.' The bones are affected by syphilis (*Timon of Athens* IV. iii. 151-2), the
conceit being that hollow things give off a hollow *sound*.

VINDICE
    And therefore I'll put on that knave for once,
    And be a right man then, a man o' the time,
    For to be honest is not to be i' the world.
    Brother I'll be that strange composèd fellow.   95
HIPPOLITO
    And I'll prefer you brother.
VINDICE   Go to then,
    The small'st advantage fattens wrongèd men.
    It may point out Occasion; if I meet her
    I'll hold her by the fore-top fast enough
    Or like the French mole heave up hair and all.   100
    I have a habit that will fit it quaintly –
    Here comes our mother.

              [Enter GRATIANA *and* CASTIZA]

HIPPOLITO   And sister.
VINDICE   We must coin.
    Women are apt you know to take false money,
    But I dare stake my soul for these two creatures,
    Only excuse excepted, that they'll swallow   105
    Because their sex is easy in belief.
GRATIANA
    What news from Court son Carlo?
HIPPOLITO   Faith mother,
    'Tis whispered there the duchess' youngest son
    Has played a rape on Lord Antonio's wife.
GRATIANA
    On that religious lady!   110
CASTIZA
    Royal blood monster! He deserves to die,
    If Italy had no more hopes but he.
VINDICE
    Sister y'ave sentenced most direct, and true,

---

92 *put on* disguise myself as
96 *prefer* recommend
100 *French mole* The mole undermines a lawn as syphilis (the French disease, proverbially) causes hair to fall out.
101 *habit* costume
102 *coin* feign (with subsequent pun on 'make money')
107 *Carlo* Presumably the author changed the character's name to 'Hippolito' in the course of composition, but forgot to cancel it here.
111 *royal blood monster* i.e., the Younger Son

    The Law's a woman, and would she were you.
    Mother I must take leave of you.
GRATIANA   Leave for what?   115
VINDICE
    I intend speedy travel.
HIPPOLITO
    That he does madam.
GRATIANA   Speedy indeed!
VINDICE
    For since my worthy father's funeral,
    My life's unnatural to me, e'en compelled,
    As if I lived now when I should be dead.   120
GRATIANA
    Indeed he was a worthy gentleman
    Had his estate been fellow to his mind.
VINDICE
    The duke did much deject him.
GRATIANA   Much?
VINDICE   Too much.
    And through disgrace oft smothered in his spirit
    When it would mount. Surely I think he died   125
    Of discontent, the nobleman's consumption.
GRATIANA
    Most sure he did.
VINDICE   Did he? 'Lack, – you know all,
    You were his midnight secretary.
GRATIANA   No,
    He was too wise to trust me with his thoughts.
VINDICE
    [*Aside*] I' faith then father thou wast wise indeed,   130
    'Wives are but made to go to bed and feed'. –
    Come mother, sister; you'll bring me onward, brother?
HIPPOLITO
    I will.
VINDICE
    [*Aside*] I'll quickly turn into another.   *Exeunt*

---

114 *the Law's a woman* Justice is conventionally represented as a blindfold woman
    holding a sword and scales.
118–20 The analogy with Hamlet seems clear and deliberate.
128 *midnight secretary* most private confidante
134 *turn into another* adopt my disguise

[Act I, Scene ii]

Enter the old DUKE, LUSSURIOSO *his son, the* DUCHESS, [SPURIO]
the bastard, the duchess' two sons AMBITIOSO *and* SUPERVACUO,
the third her youngest brought out with officers for the [*trial for*]
rape, [*and*] *two judges*

DUKE

   Duchess it is your youngest son, we're sorry,
   His violent act has e'en draw blood of honour
   And stained our honours,
   Thrown ink upon the forehead of our state
   Which envious spirits will dip their pens into   5
   After our death, and blot us in our tombs.
   For that which would seem treason in our lives
   Is laughter when we're dead. Who dares now whisper
   That dares not then speak out, and e'en proclaim
   With loud words and broad pens our closest shame.   10

1 JUDGE

   Your Grace hath spoke like to your silver years
   Full of confirmed gravity; for what is it to have
   A flattering false insculption on a tomb
   And in men's hearts reproach? The 'bowelled corpse
   May be cered in, but, with free tongue I speak –   15
   'The faults of great men through their cere cloths break'.

DUKE

   They do, we're sorry for't, it is our fate,
   To live in fear and die to live in hate.
   I leave him to your sentence: doom him, lords,
   The fact is great – whilst I sit by and sigh.   20

DUCHESS

   [*Kneels*] My gracious lord I pray be merciful
   Although his trespass far exceed his years;
   Think him to be your own as I am yours,
   Call him not son-in-law: the law I fear
   Will fall too soon upon his name and him.   25
   Temper his fault with pity.

4 *thrown . . . forehead* Compare other allusions to the forehead at lines 33, 107,
   175, and 200, and at I. iii. 8 and II. ii. 163 below.
10 *closest* most secret
13 *insculption* inscription carved into stone
14 *'bowelled* disembowelled and embalmed
15 *cered* sealed up in waxed (cered) cloth
20 *fact* crime
24 *son-in-law* step-son

LUSSURIOSO   Good my lord,
  Then 'twill not taste so bitter and unpleasant
  Upon the judge's palate; for offences
  Gilt o'er with mercy show like fairest women,
  Good only for their beauties, which washed off,   30
  No sin is uglier.
AMBITIOSO   I beseech your Grace,
  Be soft and mild, let not relentless Law
  Look with an iron forehead on our brother.
SPURIO
  [*Aside*] He yields small comfort yet – hope he shall die;
  And if a bastard's wish might stand in force,   35
  Would all the Court were turned into a corse.
DUCHESS
  No pity yet? Must I rise fruitless then –
  A wonder in a woman – are my knees
  Of such low metal that without respect –
1 JUDGE
  Let the offender stand forth,   40
  'Tis the duke's pleasure that impartial doom
  Shall take fast hold of his unclean attempt.
  A rape! Why 'tis the very core of lust,
  Double adultery.
YOUNGER SON   So sir.
2 JUDGE   And which was worse,
  Committed on the Lord Antonio's wife,   45
  That general-honest lady. Confess my lord:
  What moved you to't?
YOUNGER SON   Why flesh and blood my lord:
  What should move men unto a woman else?
LUSSURIOSO
  Oh do not jest thy doom, trust not an axe
  Or sword too far; the Law is a wise serpent   50
  And quickly can beguile thee of thy life.
  Though marriage only has made thee my brother
  I love thee so far: play not with thy death.

30–1 ed. (*one line in* Q)
36 *corse* an early form of 'corpse'
37 *rise fruitless* i.e., because she has kneeled in vain, with a pun on rise=swell in pregnancy
38–9 *are . . . respect* i.e., is not my birth noble enough to deserve respect for my plea, especially when it is made kneeling?
41 *doom* judgement
42 *fast* Dodsley (first Q)
46 *general-honest* wholly virtuous. For other composite forms see cruel-wise (line 70) and old-cool (line 74).

YOUNGER SON
   I thank you troth, good admonitions faith,
   If I'd the grace now to make use of them.   55
1 JUDGE
   That lady's name has spread such a fair wing
   Over all Italy that if our tongues
   Were sparing toward the fact, judgement itself
   Would be condemned and suffer in men's thoughts.
YOUNGER SON
   Well then 'tis done, and it would please me well   60
   Were it to do again. Sure she's a goddess
   For I'd no power to see her and to live;
   It falls out true in this for I must die.
   Her beauty was ordained to be my scaffold,
   And yet methinks I might be easier ceas'd;   65
   My fault being sport, let me but die in jest.
1 JUDGE
   This be the sentence –
DUCHESS
   Oh keep't upon your tongue, let it not slip,
   Death too soon steals out of a lawyer's lip,
   Be not so cruel-wise.
1 JUDGE   Your Grace must pardon us,   70
   'Tis but the justice of the Law.
DUCHESS   The Law
   Is grown more subtle than a woman should be.
SPURIO
   [*Aside*] Now, now he dies, rid 'em away.
DUCHESS
   [*Aside*] Oh what it is to have an old-cool duke
   To be as slack in tongue as in performance.   75
1 JUDGE
   Confirmed, this be the doom irrevocable.
DUCHESS
   Oh!
1 JUDGE   Tomorrow early –
DUCHESS   Pray be abed my lord.
1 JUDGE
   Your Grace much wrongs yourself.

57–8 *our tongues . . . fact* we punished the crime lightly
65 *ceas'd* put a stop to (Dodsley's emendation *'sess'd*=judged)
75 *performance* sexual performance

AMBITIOSO   No 'tis that tongue,
    Your too much right does do us too much wrong.
1 JUDGE
    Let that offender –
DUCHESS   Live, and be in health.   80
1 JUDGE
    Be on a scaffold –
DUKE   Hold, hold, my lord.
SPURIO [*Aside*]   Pox on't.
    What makes my dad speak now?
DUKE
    We will defer the judgement till next sitting,
    In the meantime let him be kept close prisoner:
    Guard bear him hence.
AMBITIOSO [*Aside*]   Brother this makes for thee,   85
    Fear not, we'll have a trick to set thee free.
YOUNGER SON
    [*Aside*] Brother I will expect it from you both,
    And in that hope I rest.
SUPERVACUO   Farewell, be merry.
                              Exit [YOUNGER SON] *with a guard*
SPURIO
    Delayed, deferred, nay then if Judgement have
    Cold blood, flattery and bribes will kill it.   90
DUKE
    About it then my lords with your best powers,
    More serious business calls upon our hours.
                              Exeunt; manet DUCHESS
DUCHESS
    Was't ever known step-duchess was so mild
    And calm as I? Some now would plot his death
    With easy doctors, those loose living men,   95
    And make his withered Grace fall to his grave
    And keep church better.
    Some second wife would do this, and dispatch
    Her double loathèd lord at meat and sleep.
    Indeed 'tis true an old man's twice a child,   100
    Mine cannot speak! One of his single words
    Would quite have freed my youngest dearest son
    From death or durance, and have made him walk

---

79 *too much right* too strict application of the law, or too great privilege as a judge
89–90 ed. (Delayed . . . bloud / Flattery . . . it / Q)
95 *easy* compliant
103 *durance* imprisonment

With a bold foot upon the thorny law,
Whose prickles should bow under him; but 't 'as not: 105
And therefore wedlock faith shall be forgot.
I'll kill him in his forehead, hate there feed –
That wound is deepest though it never bleed;

[*Enter* SPURIO]

And here comes he whom my heart points unto,
His bastard son, but my love's true-begot;   110
Many a wealthy letter have I sent him
Swelled up with jewels, and the timorous man
Is yet but coldly kind;
That jewel's mine that quivers in his ear,
Mocking his master's chillness and vain fear –   115
H'as spied me now.
SPURIO   Madam? Your Grace so private?
My duty on your hand.
DUCHESS
Upon my hand sir, troth I think you'd fear
To kiss my hand too if my lip stood there.
SPURIO
Witness I would not madam.   [*He kisses her*]
DUCHESS   'Tis a wonder,   120
For ceremony has made many fools.
It is as easy way unto a duchess
As to a hatted dame, if her love answer,
But that by timorous honours, pale respects,
Idle degrees of fear, men make their ways   125
Hard of themselves. What have you thought of me?
SPURIO
Madam I ever think of you, in duty,
Regard and –
DUCHESS   Puh, upon my love I mean.
SPURIO
I would 'twere love, but 't 'as a fouler name
Than lust; you are my father's wife, your Grace may guess
        now   130
What I could call it.
DUCHESS   Why th'art his son but falsely,
'Tis a hard question whether he begot thee.

---

105 *'t 'as* ed. ('tis Q) i.e., 'it, one of the duke's words, has'
117 *My duty . . . hand* in token of dutiful respect I kiss your hand
123 *hatted dame* Women of the lower class wore hats.
125 *Idle* foolish

SPURIO

    I' faith 'tis true too; I'm an uncertain man
    Of more uncertain woman; may be his groom
    O' the stable begot me – you know I know not.   135
    He could ride a horse well, a shrewd suspicion – marry!
    He was wondrous tall, he had his length i' faith
    For peeping over half-shut holiday windows:
    Men would desire him 'light. When he was afoot
    He made a goodly show under a penthouse,   140
    And when he rid his hat would check the signs
    And clatter barbers' basins.

DUCHESS   Nay, set you a horseback once

    You'll ne'er 'light off.

SPURIO   Indeed I am a beggar.

DUCHESS

    That's more the sign thou art great – but to our love.
    Let it stand firm both in thought and mind   145
    That the duke was thy father: as no doubt then
    He bid fair for't, thy injury is the more;
    For had he cut thee a right diamond,
    Thou had'st been next set in the dukedom's ring,
    When his worn self like Age's easy slave   150

134–5 Spurio's speculations about his paternity recall the bastard Edmund in *King Lear* who claims (I. ii. 12–15) that his father's unlawful act of begetting him 'in the lusty stealth of nature' endowed him with

    'More composition and fierce quality,
    Than doth within a dull, stale, tired bed
    Go to th'creating a whole tribe of fops,
    Got 'tween asleep and wake'

136 *ride* The verb often carried a sexual sense (= have sexual intercourse with).

137–8 Given the context, further sexual innuendoes are to be assumed here, the general sense being that he went out to attract merchants' and citizens' wives, showing off and making their husbands jealous.

139 *'light* alight (from his horse, so that he could not make eyes at their women)

140 *penthouse* awning over shop windows ('your hat penthouse-like o'er the shop of your eyes' – *Love's Labour's Lost* III. i. 17–18) or any sloping-roofed subsidiary building, covered way or arcade

141–2 He deliberately clattered the suspended shop signs and barbers' basins. (Presumably this arrogant behaviour was intended to make the shopkeepers jealous as well as to insult them. Mockery of citizens is typical in satiric plays of this time.)

142–3 Mocking Spurio's exuberant speech with a proverb (used in Jonson, *The Staple of News*, 4.1): 'Set a beggar on horse back he'll never lin till he be a gallop.'

148–9 *diamond . . . ring* This recalls the image in I. i. 19–20.

Had dropped out of the collet into the grave.
What wrong can equal this? Canst thou be tame
And think upon't?
SPURIO   No, mad and think upon't.
DUCHESS
Who would not be revenged of such a father,
E'en in the worst way? I would thank that sin   155
That could most injure him, and be in league with it.
Oh what a grief 'tis that a man should live
But once i' the world, and then to live a bastard,
The curse o' the womb, the thief of Nature,
Begot against the seventh commandment   160
Half damned in the conception by the justice
Of that unbribed everlasting law.
SPURIO
Oh I'd a hot backed devil to my father.
DUCHESS
Would not this mad e'en Patience, make blood rough?
Who but an eunuch would not sin, his bed   165
By one false minute disinherited?
SPURIO
Ay, there's the vengeance that my birth was wrapped in,
I'll be revenged for all: now hate begin,
I'll call foul incest but a venial sin.
DUCHESS
Cold still: in vain then must a duchess woo?   170
SPURIO
Madam I blush to say what I will do.
DUCHESS
Thence flew sweet comfort, earnest and farewell.
                                   [*She kisses him*]
SPURIO
Oh one incestuous kiss picks open hell.
DUCHESS
Faith now old duke, my vengeance shall reach high,
I'll arm thy brow with woman's heraldry.   *Exit* 175
SPURIO
Duke, thou did'st do me wrong and by thy act
Adultery is my nature.
Faith if the truth were known I was begot

---

151 *collet* socket, setting for a precious stone in a ring
164 *blood* i.e., temper
175 *woman's heraldry* i.e., the cuckold's horns which proverbially sprouted on the
    betrayed husband's forehead

After some gluttonous dinner – some stirring dish
Was my first father; when deep healths went round   180
And ladies cheeks were painted red with wine,
Their tongues as short and nimble as their heels
Uttering words sweet and thick; and when they rose
Were merrily disposed to fall again.
In such a whispering and withdrawing hour,   185
When base male bawds kept sentinel at stair-head
Was I stol'n softly – oh damnation met
The sin of feasts, drunken adultery.
I feel it swell me; my revenge is just,
I was begot in impudent wine and lust.   190
Stepmother I consent to thy desires,
I love thy mischief well but I hate thee,
And those three cubs thy sons, wishing confusion
Death and disgrace may be their epitaphs.
As for my brother, the duke's only son,   195
Whose birth is more beholding to report
Than mine, and yet perhaps as falsely sown
– Women must not be trusted with their own –
I'll loose my days upon him, hate all I!
Duke on thy brow I'll draw my bastardy: 200
For indeed a bastard by nature should make cuckolds
Because he is the son of a cuckold maker.   *Exit*

[Act I, Scene iii]

Enter VINDICE *and* HIPPOLITO, VINDICE *in disguise to attend*
LUSSURIOSO *the duke's son*

VINDICE
   What brother, am I far enough from myself?

179–87 Cf. Marston, *The Malcontent* III. ii. 24–49, especially
         'When in an Italian lascivious palace, a lady guardianless,
         Left to the push of all allurement . . .
         Her veins fill'd high with heating delicates,
         Soft rest, sweet music, amorous masquerers,
         Lascivious banquets, sin itself gilt o'er'.
195 *only son* i.e., Lussurioso
196 *birth . . . report* legitimacy is more firmly claimed
200 Cf. line 175 above.
   1 *far . . . myself* sufficiently well disguised

HIPPOLITO
As if another man had been sent whole
Into the world and none wist how he came.
VINDICE
It will confirm me bold – the child o' the Court;
Let blushes dwell i' the country. Impudence,   5
Thou goddess of the palace, mistress of mistresses,
To whom the costly-perfumed people pray,
Strike thou my forehead into dauntless marble,
Mine eyes to steady sapphires; turn my visage
And if I must needs glow let me blush inward   10
That this immodest season may not spy
That scholar in my cheeks, fool bashfulness,
That maid in the old time whose flush of grace
Would never suffer her to get good clothes.
Our maids are wiser and are less ashamed –   15
Save Grace the bawd I seldom hear grace named!
HIPPOLITO
Nay brother you reach out o' the verge now –

[*Enter* LUSSURIOSO]

'Sfoot, the duke's son! Settle your looks.
VINDICE
Pray let me not be doubted.
HIPPOLITO
My lord –
LUSSURIOSO Hippolito? – [*to Vindice*] Be absent, leave us.   20
                              [*Vindice withdraws*]

HIPPOLITO
My lord, after long search, wary enquiries
And politic siftings I made choice of yon fellow
Whom I guess rare for many deep employments:
This our age swims within him; and if Time
Had so much hair I should take him for Time,   25
He is so near kin to this present minute.
LUSSURIOSO
'Tis enough,
We thank thee: yet words are but great men's blanks;

16 The mother's name, Gratiana, means 'grace'.
17 i.e., now you are going too far
17–18 *prose in* Q
24–5 *Time . . . hair* Time was proverbially bald: see Tilley T 311.
28 *words . . . blanks* i.e., words come cheap. *Blanks* may mean a document or bill
    with spaces left to be filled in, or metal not yet stamped to give it value as
    currency (as Foakes suggests).

Gold though it be dumb does utter the best thanks.
                                        [*Gives him money*]

HIPPOLITO
   Your plenteous honour – an ex'lent fellow my lord.   30
LUSSURIOSO
   So, give us leave –
                                        [*Exit* HIPPOLITO]
   [*to Vindice*]   Welcome, be not far off,
   We must be better acquainted. Push, be bold
   With us, thy hand.
VINDICE   With all my heart i' faith!
   How dost sweet musk-cat? When shall we lie together?
LUSSURIOSO
   [*Aside*] Wondrous knave!   35
   Gather him into boldness: 'sfoot the slave's
   Already as familiar as an ague
   And shakes me at his pleasure – Friend I can
   Forget myself in private, but elsewhere
   I pray do you remember me.   40
VINDICE
   Oh very well sir – I conster myself saucy!
LUSSURIOSO
   What hast been – of what profession?
VINDICE
   A bone setter.
LUSSURIOSO
   A bone setter!
VINDICE
   A bawd my lord. One that sets bones together.   45
LUSSURIOSO
   [*Aside*] Notable bluntness!
   Fit, fit for me, e'en trained up to my hand. –
   Thou hast been scrivener to much knavery then?

31–4 *prose in* Q
34 *musk-cat* paramour, courtesan. Cf. Jonson, *Every Man out of his Humour*
   II. i. 97: 'He sleepes with a muske-cat every night.' Here a homosexual affair is
   implied.
36 *Gather . . . boldness* This phrase is obscure. OED 'gather' vt 16e records a rare
   meaning, 'chide or reprove'. Given the sense of the general context, where
   Lussurioso realises he made an error at lines 31–3 in supposing Vindice to be
   shy, the sense may be 'he must be accounted bold'.
39 *Forget myself* be familiar
40 i.e., kindly show me due respect
41 *conster* construe, consider
48 *scrivener* secretary, assistant

VINDICE
  Fool to abundance sir; I have been witness
  To the surrenders of a thousand virgins   50
  And not so little;
  I have seen patrimonies washed apieces,
  Fruit fields turned into bastards,
  And in a world of acres
  Not so much dust due to the heir 'twas left to   55
  As would well gravel a petition.
LUSSURIOSO
  [Aside] Fine villain! Troth I like him wondrously,
  He's e'en shaped for my purpose. – Then thou know'st
  In the world strange lust?
VINDICE   Oh Dutch lust! Fulsome lust!
  Drunken procreation, which begets so many drunkards;   60
  Some father dreads not, gone to bed in wine,
  To slide from the mother and cling the daughter-in-law;
  Some uncles are adulterous with their nieces,
  Brothers with brothers' wives – Oh hour of incest!
  Any kin now next to the rim o' the sister   65
  Is man's meat in these days, and in the morning,
  When they are up and dressed and their mask on,
  Who can perceive this, save that eternal eye
  That sees through flesh and all? Well – if anything be
      damned
  It will be twelve o'clock at night: that twelve   70
  Will never 'scape;
  It is the Judas of the hours, wherein
  Honest salvation is betrayed to sin.
LUSSURIOSO
  In troth it is too; but let this talk glide.
  It is our blood to err though hell gaped loud: 75
  Ladies know Lucifer fell, yet still are proud!

49 *Fool* Q's reading means 'voluntary dupe' (Nicoll). Collins in his 1878 edition
    conjectures *'Sfoot*, and some such expletive (*Pooh, Push*) is orthographically
    possible.
52 *patrimonies washed apieces* estates dissolved or broken up by drunken
    profligacy (The metaphor associates drinking with flooding.)
53 *fruit fields ... bastards* i.e., fruit fields sold to pay for maintaining bastards,
    sexual profligacy being another threat to maintaining estates. County gentry
    selling out to city merchants are often a topic of satiric comment in plays of the
    time, especially Middleton's city comedies.
56 *gravel* Sand would be strewn on a petition to dry the ink.
59 *Dutch* i.e., proverbially excessive, Gargantuan
61-2 ed. (Some ... mother / And ... daughter-in-law / Q)

Now sir, wert thou as secret as thou'rt subtle
And deeply fathomed into all estates
I would embrace thee for a near employment,
And thou should'st swell in money and be able   80
To make lame beggars crouch to thee.
VINDICE   My lord?
Secret? I ne'er had that disease o' the mother,
I praise my father! Why are men made close
But to keep thoughts in best? I grant you this:
Tell but some woman a secret over night,   85
Your doctor may find it in the urinal i' the morning;
But, my lord –
LUSSURIOSO   So, thou'rt confirmed in me
And thus I enter thee.   [*Gives him money*]
VINDICE   This Indian devil
Will quickly enter any man: but a usurer,
He prevents that by entering the devil first!   90
LUSSURIOSO
Attend me, I am past my depth in lust
And I must swim or drown. All my desires
Are levelled at a virgin not far from Court,
To whom I have conveyed by messenger
Many waxed lines full of my neatest spirit,   95
And jewels that were able to ravish her
Without the help of man: all which and more
She, foolish-chaste, sent back, the messengers
Receiving frowns for answers.
VINDICE   Possible?
'Tis a rare Phoenix whoe'er she be,   100
If your desires be such, she so repugnant:
In troth my lord I'd be revenged and marry her.
LUSSURIOSO
Push; the dowry of her blood and of her fortunes
Are both too mean – good enough to be bad withal.
I'm one of that number can defend   105
Marriage is good; yet rather keep a friend.

---

82 *disease o' the mother* i.e., of talking too much, with a possible pun on 'the
   mother', a term for a form of hysteria, as in *King Lear* II.iv. 56
87 *in me* in my confidence
88 *Indian devil* silver and gold from the Indies
95 *waxed lines* sealed letters
   neatest most intense
98 *foolish-chaste* Cf. composite adjectives in I.ii. 46 and n.
101 *repugnant* resisting
106 *friend* mistress

Give me my bed by stealth – there's true delight;
What breeds a loathing in't but night by night?
LUSSURIOSO
VINDICE
A very fine religion!
LUSSURIOSO Therefore thus:
I'll trust thee in the business of my heart 110
Because I see thee well experienced
In this luxurious day wherein we breathe:
Go thou and with a smooth enchanting tongue
Bewitch her ears and cozen her of all grace;
Enter upon the portion of her soul, 115
Her honour, which she calls her chastity,
And bring it into expense, for honesty
Is like a stock of money laid to sleep
Which, ne'er so little broke, does never keep.
VINDICE
You have given it the tang i' faith my lord; 120
Make known the lady to me and my brain
Shall swell with strange invention: I will move it
Till I expire with speaking and drop down
Without a word to save me; – but I'll work –
LUSSURIOSO
We thank thee and will raise thee; receive her name. 125
It is the only daughter to Madam Gratiana
The late widow.
VINDICE [*Aside*] Oh, my sister, my sister!
LUSSURIOSO
Why dost walk aside?
VINDICE
My lord I was thinking how I might begin,
As thus – 'oh lady' – or twenty hundred devices: 130
Her very bodkin will put a man in.
LUSSURIOSO
Ay, or the wagging of her hair.
VINDICE
No, that shall put you in my lord.

115–16 A bride brings to her husband a financial dowry; she also brings a spiritual
  dowry, virtue, and its corresponding social/cultural value, honour.
117 *bring . . . expense* make her spend it
120 *given it* ed. (*gint* Q)
  given it the tang caught the flavour, got it right
122 *move it* make it work
129–31 *prose in* Q
131 *put a man in* provide an opening for seduction

LUSSURIOSO
  Shall't? Why content: dost know the daughter then?
VINDICE
  Oh ex'lent well by sight.
LUSSURIOSO   That was her brother   135
  That did prefer thee to us.
VINDICE   My lord I think so,
  I knew I had seen him somewhere.
LUSSURIOSO
  And therefore prithee let thy heart to him
  Be as a virgin, close.
VINDICE   Oh my good lord.
LUSSURIOSO
  We may laugh at that simple age within him –   140
VINDICE
  Ha! Ha! Ha!
LUSSURIOSO
  Himself being made the subtle instrument
  To wind up a good fellow.
VINDICE   That's I my lord.
LUSSURIOSO
  That's thou.
  To entice and work his sister.
VINDICE   A pure novice!   145
LUSSURIOSO
  'Twas finely managed.
VINDICE   Gallantly carried:
  A pretty-perfumed villian!
LUSSURIOSO   I've bethought me.
  If she prove chaste still and immoveable,
  Venture upon the mother, and with gifts
  As I will furnish thee, begin with her.   150
VINDICE
  Oh fie, fie, that's the wrong end my lord.
  'Tis mere impossible that a mother by any gifts
  Should become a bawd to her own daughter!
LUSSURIOSO
  Nay then I see thou'rt but a puny
  In the subtle mystery of a woman: 155
  Why 'tis held now no dainty dish: the name

142-3 Lussurioso here subtly devises a plan in which the brother unknowingly is to
    become instrumental in the corrupting of his own sister.
143 *wind up* set up, recruit (with the implication of embolden)
152-7 *prose in* Q

Is so in league with age that nowadays
It does eclipse three quarters of a mother.
VINDICE
Does it so my lord?
Let me alone then to eclipse the fourth.   160
LUSSURIOSO
Why well said; come I'll furnish thee: but first
Swear to be true in all.
VINDICE   True?
LUSSURIOSO   Nay but swear!
VINDICE
Swear?
I hope your honour little doubts my faith.
LUSSURIOSO
Yet, for my humour's sake, 'cause I love swearing –   165
VINDICE
'Cause you love swearing, 'slud I will.
LUSSURIOSO   Why enough:
Ere long look to be made of better stuff.
VINDICE
That will do well indeed my lord.
LUSSURIOSO   Attend me.   [Exit]
VINDICE
Oh, Now let me burst, I've eaten noble poison!
We are made strange fellows, brother, innocent villains: 170
Wilt not be angry when thou hear'st on't, think'st thou?
I' faith thou shalt. Swear me to foul my sister!
Sword I durst make a promise of him to thee,
Thou shalt dis-heir him, it shall be thine honour;
And yet, now angry froth is down in me,   175
It would not prove the meanest policy
In this disguise to try the faith of both;
Another might have had the self-same office,
Some slave that would have wrought effectually,
Ay and perhaps o'erwrought 'em: therefore I,   180
Being thought travelled, will apply myself
Unto the self-same form, forget my nature,
As if no part about me were kin to 'em,
So touch 'em – though I durst almost for good
Venture my lands in heaven upon their blood.   Exit 185

153 This is what happens in Machiavelli's comedy *Mandragola*.
161–4 ed. (*prose in* Q)
167 i.e., expect promotion as your prompt reward
181 *travelled* on a journey abroad

[Act I, Scene iv]

Enter the discontented lord ANTONIO (*whose wife the duchess'*
youngest son ravished); *he discovering* [*her dead body*] *to*
certain lords and [*to* PIERO *and*] HIPPOLITO

ANTONIO
　　Draw nearer lords and be sad witnesses
　　Of a fair comely building newly fallen,
　　Being falsely undermined. Violent rape
　　Has played a glorious act: behold my lords
　　A sight that strikes man out of me.   5
PIERO
　　That virtuous lady!
ANTONIO　　　　　　　Precedent for wives!
HIPPOLITO
　　The blush of many women, whose chaste presence
　　Would e'en call shame up to their cheeks
　　And make pale wanton sinners have good colours –
ANTONIO
　　Dead!   10
　　Her honour first drank poison, and her life,
　　Being fellows in one house, did pledge her honour.
PIERO
　　Oh grief of many!
ANTONIO　　　　　I marked not this before:
　　A prayer book the pillow to her cheek;
　　This was her rich confection, and another   15
　　Placed in her right hand with a leaf tucked up,
　　Pointing to these words:
　　Melius virtute mori, quam per dedecus vivere.
　　True and effectual it is indeed.

---

0 sd Presumably a traverse curtain, hung across the central part of the tiring
　　house wall, is drawn to reveal the dead woman: her pose is emblematic and its
　　significance is explained by the lords who gather round it. Its pose is like that of
　　Imogen, who falls asleep, leaving a book open at a significant place, in
　　Cymbeline II. ii. See also the discussion in Marion Lomax, *Stage Images and*
　　Traditions, Shakespeare to Ford (1987).
15 *confection* a term for a medicinal means of preservation, here transferred to a
　　religious sense
18 'Better die virtuous than live dishonoured.' This classical Roman principle
　　inspired the tragic resolve of the noble Lucrece, who committed suicide to
　　purify the family honour after being raped by Tarquin – a tale which
　　Shakespeare treated in his poem *The Rape of Lucrece*.

HIPPOLITO

My lord since you invite us to your sorrows   20
Let's truly taste 'em, that with equal comfort
As to ourselves we may relieve your wrongs:
We have grief too that yet walks without tongue:
Curae leves loquuntur, majores stupent.

ANTONIO

You deal with truth my lord.   25
Lend me but your attentions and I'll cut
Long grief into short words: last revelling night,
When torchlight made an artificial noon
About the Court, some courtiers in the masque
Putting on better faces than their own,   30
Being full of fraud and flattery, amongst whom
The duchess' youngest son – that moth to honour –
Filled up a room; and with long lust to eat
Into my wearing, amongst all the ladies
Singled out that dear form, who ever lived   35
As cold in lust as she is now in death –
Which that step-duchess' monster knew too well –
And therefore in the height of all the revels,
When music was heard loudest, courtiers busiest,
And ladies great with laughter – Oh vicious minute!   40
Unfit, but for relation, to be spoke of –
Then with a face more impudent than his vizard
He harried her amidst a throng of pandars
That live upon damnation of both kinds
And fed the ravenous vulture of his lust.   45
Oh death to think on't! She, her honour forced,
Deemed it a nobler dowry for her name
To die with poison than to live with shame.

HIPPOLITO

A wondrous lady of rare fire compact,
She's made her name an empress by that act.   50

PIERO

My lord what judgement follows the offender?

24 'Lesser cares can speak, greater cares are silent'. Nicoll notes this as a
   recollection of Seneca, *Hippolytus*.
29 *masque* Q (mask)
32 *moth* The younger son destroys Antonio's honour as a moth eats away fabric.
   Antonio refers to his honour as clothing ('my wearing', line 34).
37 *step-duchess' monster* ed. (step Duchess-Monster Q)
39 *heard* ed. (hard Q)
41 *for relation* except for the necessity of informing you
50 *empress* There may be a pun on 'impress' = emblem.

ANTONIO
Faith none my lord, it cools and is deferred.
PIERO
Delay the doom for rape?
ANTONIO
Oh you must note who 'tis should die –
The duchess' son. She'll look to be a saver: 55
'Judgement in this age is near kin to favour'.
HIPPOLITO
Nay then, step forth thou bribeless officer;
                                        [*Draws sword*]
I bind you all in steel to bind you surely,
Here let your oaths meet, to be kept and paid
Which else will stick like rust and shame the blade.   60
Strengthen my vow, that if at the next sitting
Judgement speak all in gold and spare the blood
Of such a serpent, e'en before their seats
To let his soul out, which long since was found
Guilty in heaven.
ALL   We swear it and will act it.   65
ANTONIO
Kind gentlemen I thank you in mine ire.
HIPPOLITO
'Twere pity
The ruins of so fair a monument
Should not be dipped in the defacer's blood.
PIERO
Her funeral shall be wealthy, for her name   70
Merits a tomb of pearl. My lord Antonio
For this time wipe your lady from your eyes;
No doubt our grief and yours may one day court it
When we are more familiar with Revenge.
ANTONIO
That is my comfort gentlemen, and I joy   75
In this one happiness above the rest,
Which will be called a miracle at last,
That being an old man I'd a wife so chaste.   *Exeunt*

---

59 Ironically recalling I. iii. 160–75 above, and probably intending a recognisable
   allusion to *Hamlet* I. v.

Act II, Scene i

Enter CASTIZA *the sister*

CASTIZA

How hardly shall that maiden be beset
Whose only fortunes are her constant thoughts,
That has no other child's-part but her honour
That keeps her low and empty in estate.
Maids and their honours are like poor beginners:　　　　5
Were not sin rich there would be fewer sinners:
Why had not virtue a revenue? Well,
I know the cause: 'twould have impoverished hell.

[*Enter* DONDOLO]

How now Dondolo.

DONDOLO

Madonna, there is one as they say a thing of flesh and　　10
blood, a man I take him, by his beard, that would very
desirously mouth to mouth with you.

CASTIZA

What's that?

DONDOLO

Show his teeth in your company.

CASTIZA

I understand thee not.　　　　15

DONDOLO

Why, speak with you Madonna.

CASTIZA

Why, say so madman and cut off a great deal of dirty way.
Had it not been better spoke, in ordinary words, that one
would speak with me?

DONDOLO

Ha, ha, that's as ordinary as two shillings; I would strive a　　20
little to show myself in my place. A gentleman-usher scorns
to use the phrase and fancy of a servingman.

CASTIZA

Yours be your own sir; go direct him hither.

[*Exit* DONDOLO]

I hope some happy tidings from my brother

---

1 *beset* beseiged, surrounded by men of hostile intent
3 *child's-part* inheritance
23 *own* ed. (one Q)

That lately travelled, whom my soul affects.   25
Here he comes.

Enter VINDICE *her brother disguised*

VINDICE
Lady the best of wishes to your sex:
Fair skins and new gowns.   [*Gives her a letter*]
CASTIZA   Oh they shall thank you sir –
Whence this?
VINDICE   Oh from a dear and worthy friend,
Mighty!
CASTIZA   From whom?
VINDICE   The duke's son.
CASTIZA   Receive that!   30
A box o' the ear to [VINDICE] *her brother*
I swore I'd put anger in my hand
And pass the virgin limits of myself
To him that next appeared in that base office,
To be his sin's attorney. Bear to him
That figure of my hate upon thy cheek   35
Whilst 'tis yet hot, and I'll reward thee for't;
Tell him my honour shall have a rich name
When several harlots shall share his with shame:
Farewell, commend me to him in my hate!   *Exit*
VINDICE
It is the sweetest box that e'er my nose came nigh: 40
The finest drawn-work cuff that e'er was worn:
I'll love this blow forever, and this cheek
Shall still henceforward take the wall of this.
Oh I'm above my tongue! Most constant sister,
In this thou hast right honourable shown;   45
Many are called by their honour that have none,
Thou art approved forever in my thoughts.
It is not in the power of words to taint thee,
And yet for the salvation of my oath,
As my resolve in that point, I will lay   50
Hard siege unto my mother, though I know
A siren's tongue could not bewitch her so.

[*Enter* GRATIANA]

25 *affects* loves
40 ed. (It . . . box / That . . . nigh / Q)
41 *drawn-work cuff* a pun on (i) the decorated cuff of her sleeve, (ii) the blow or
     cuff round the ear she gave him which has decorated his cheek (Foakes)
43 *take the wall* take precedence over

Mass, fitly, here she comes: thanks my disguise:
Madam good afternoon.
GRATIANA   Y'are welcome sir.
VINDICE
The next of Italy commends him to you: 55
Our mighty expectation, the duke's son.
GRATIANA
I think myself much honoured that he pleases
To rank me in his thoughts.
VINDICE   So may you lady:
One that is like to be our sudden duke –
The crown gapes for him every tide – and then   60
Commander o'er us all; do but think on him,
How blest were they now that could pleasure him,
E'en with anything almost.
GRATIANA   Ay, save their honour.
VINDICE
Tut, one would let a little of that go too
And ne'er be seen in't: ne'er be seen in't, mark you.   65
I'd wink and let it go –
GRATIANA   Marry but I would not.
VINDICE
Marry but I would I hope; I know you would too
If you'd that blood now which you gave your daughter;
To her indeed 'tis, this wheel comes about;
That man that must be all this perhaps ere morning   70
– For his white father does but mould away –
Has long desired your daughter.
GRATIANA   Desired?
VINDICE
Nay but hear me:
He desires now that will command hereafter,
Therefore be wise; I speak as more a friend   75
To you than him. Madam I know y'are poor,
And 'lack the day,
There are too many poor ladies already;
Why should you vex the number? 'Tis despised.
Live wealthy, rightly understand the world   80
And chide away that foolish country girl
Keeps company with your daughter, chastity.

55 *next of Italy* i.e., next in succession to the Duke
65 *in't* i.e., losing honour
77-8 *one line in* Q
79 *vex* aggravate the problem by increasing the number

GRATIANA

Oh fie, fie, the riches of the world cannot hire
A mother to such a most unnatural task.

VINDICE

No, but a thousand angels can.   85
Men have no power, angels must work you to it,
The world descends into such base born evils
That forty angels can make four score devils.
There will be fools still I perceive, still fools.
Would I be poor, dejected, scorned of greatness,   90
Swept from the palace, and see other daughters
Spring with the dew o'the Court, having mine own
So much desired and loved – by the duke's son!
No, I would raise my state upon her breast
And call her eyes my tenants; I would count   95
My yearly maintenance upon her cheeks,
Take coach upon her lip, and all her parts
Should keep men after men and I would ride
In pleasure upon pleasure.
You took great pains for her, once when it was,   100
Let her requite it now, though it be but some.
You brought her forth, she may well bring you home.

GRATIANA

Oh heavens, this overcomes me!

VINDICE

[*Aside*] Not, I hope, already?

GRATIANA

[*Aside*] It is too strong for me. Men know, that know us,   105
We are so weak their words can overthrow us.
He touched me nearly, made my virtues bate
When his tongue struck upon my poor estate.

85 *angels* gold coins

90 *dejected* lowly

95-9 The daughter's physical attractions are itemised and fancifully imagined as parts of an estate, each part yielding rents to pay for the mother's extravagant way of life. This is an ironic use of a rhetorical scheme, the poetical catalogue of the charms of a woman from head to foot: see Andrew Marvell's poem 'To His Coy Mistress' for a comic-hyperbolic version, in which each part of the body is valued in terms of the time needed to admire it as it deserves:

'An hundred years should go to praise
Thine eyes, and on thy forehead gaze.
Two hundred to adore each breast . . .'

98 *ride* with a bawdy innuendo, as at I. ii. 136

100 *pains* i.e., in childbirth as well as those taken in careful upbringing

101 *but some* i.e, only in part

107 *bate* become depressed, weaken

VINDICE
    [*Aside*] I e'en quake to proceed, my spirit turns edge,
    I fear me she's unmothered, yet I'll venture –   110
    'That woman is all male whom none can enter!'
    What think you now lady, speak, are you wiser?
    What said advancement to you? Thus it said:
    The daughter's fall lifts up the mother's head:
    Did it not madam? But I'll swear it does   115
    In many places. Tut, this age fears no man –
    ''Tis no shame to be bad, because 'tis common.'
GRATIANA
    Ay that's the comfort on't.
VINDICE   The comfort on't!
    I keep the best for last; can these persuade you
    To forget heaven – and –   [*Gives her gold*]
GRATIANA   Ay, these are they –
VINDICE   Oh! –   120
GRATIANA
    That enchant our sex; these are the means
    That govern our affections. That woman will
    Not be troubled with the mother long
    That sees the comfortable shine of you;
    I blush to think what for your sakes I'll do.   125
VINDICE
    [*Aside*] Oh suffering heaven with thy invisible finger

---

109 *turns edge* becomes blunt or dull
116 *places*, ed. (places. Q)
117 *'tis common* Perhaps recalling *Hamlet* I. ii. 72–4:
      Gertrude Thou know'st 'tis common, all that lives must die,
                    Passing through nature to eternity.
    Hamlet   Ay, madam, it is common.
121–2 ed. (That . . . sexe / These . . . woman / Q)
123 *the mother* Punning on the senses (i) a mother's sense of duty, (ii) hysteria, as at
    I. iii. 80.
125 *blush* another emphasis on this sign of modest or guilty shame (See IV. iv. 44.)
126 *invisible finger* Probably, taken with other references to supernatural omens in
    the play (the blazing star, V. iii. 16; the thunder, IV. ii. 159, 198), the dramatist
    has in mind the Book of Daniel, chapter 5, the story of Belshazzar, who (with a
    thousand of his lords) made a great feast and praised the gods of gold and silver,
    brass, iron, wood and stone while drinking wine. Then 'came forth fingers of a
    man's hand' and wrote on the wall. The king saw this and trembled. Daniel,
    called to interpret the words (Mene, Mene, Tekel, Upharsin), declared that
    they announced God's judgement that Belshazzar's rule was found wanting and
    his kingdom would be divided. The same night Belshazzar the king was slain
    and Darius the Median took his kingdom. The phrase 'the finger of God' occurs
    in Exodus 8:19 and Luke 11:20.

E'en at this instant turn the precious side
Of both mine eyeballs inward, not to see myself.
GRATIANA
　Look you sir.
VINDICE　　　　　Holla.
GRATIANA　　　　　　　　Let this thank your pains.
VINDICE
　Oh you're a kind madam.　　　　　　　　　　　130
GRATIANA
　I'll see how I can move.
VINDICE　　　　　　　　　Your words will sting.
GRATIANA
　If she be still chaste I'll ne'er call her mine.
VINDICE
　[Aside] Spoke truer than you meant it.
GRATIANA
　Daughter Castiza.

[Enter CASTIZA]

CASTIZA　　　　　Madam.
VINDICE　　　　　　　　　Oh she's yonder.
　Meet her.　　　　　　　　　　　　　　　135
　Troops of celestial soldiers guard her heart:
　Yon dam has devils enough to take her part.
CASTIZA
　Madam what makes yon evil-officed man
　In presence of you?
GRATIANA　　　　　Why?
CASTIZA　　　　　　　　He lately brought
　Immodest writing sent from the duke's son　　　140
　To tempt me to dishonourable act.
GRATIANA
　Dishonourable act? Good honourable fool,
　That wouldst be honest 'cause thou wouldst be so,
　Producing no one reason but thy will;
　And 't'as a good report, prettily commended –　　145
　But pray by whom? Mean people, ignorant people!
　The better sort I'm sure cannot abide it,
　And by what rule should we square out our lives
　But by our betters' actions? Oh if thou knew'st
　What 'twere to lose it, thou would never keep it:　　150

134–5 *one line in* Q
147 *better* i.e., superior in wealth and rank. Note this attempt to suppress the moral
　　connotation.

But there's a cold curse laid upon all maids,
Whilst others clip the sun they clasp the shades!
Virginity is paradise, locked up.
You cannot come by yourselves without fee,
And 'twas decreed that man should keep the key: 155
Deny advancement, treasure, the duke's son!
CASTIZA
I cry you mercy; lady I mistook you,
Pray did you see my mother? Which way went you?
Pray God I have not lost her.
VINDICE [*Aside*]   Prettily put by.
GRATIANA
Are you as proud to me as coy to him?   160
Do you not know me now?
CASTIZA   Why are you she?
The world's so changed, one shape into another,
It is a wise child now that knows her mother.
VINDICE
[*Aside*] Most right i' faith.
GRATIANA   I owe your cheek my hand
For that presumption now, but I'll forget it;   165
Come you shall leave those childish 'haviours
And understand your time; fortunes flow to you
– What, will you be a girl?
If all feared drowning that spy waves ashore
Gold would grow rich and all the merchants poor.   170
CASTIZA
It is a pretty saying of a wicked one,
But methinks now
It does not show so well out of your mouth –
Better in his.
VINDICE [*Aside*] Faith bad enough in both
Were I in earnest – as I'll seem no less. –   175
I wonder lady your own mother's words
Cannot be taken, nor stand in full force.
'Tis honesty you urge: what's honesty?
'Tis but heaven's beggar; and what woman is
So foolish to keep honesty   180
And be not able to keep herself? No,
Times are grown wiser and will keep less charge.

154 i.e., you cannot take full possession of yourselves without paying a fee to have
    the treasure unlocked
163 a proverb listed by Tilley (C 309)
171–2 *one line in* Q
179–80 *one line in* Q

A maid that has small portion now intends
To break up house and live upon her friends;
How blest are you: you have happiness alone; 185
Others must fall to thousands, you to one
Sufficient in himself to make your forehead
Dazzle the world with jewels, and petitionary people
Start at your presence.

GRATIANA   Oh if I were young
I should be ravished!

CASTIZA   Ay, to lose your honour. 190

VINDICE
'Slid, how can you lose your honour
To deal with my lord's grace?
He'll add more honour to it by his title;
Your mother will tell you how.

GRATIANA   That I will.

VINDICE
Oh think upon the pleasure of the palace, 195
Securèd ease and state; the stirring meats
Ready to move out of the dishes
That e'en now quicken when they're eaten;
Banquets abroad by torchlight, musics, sports,
Bare-headed vassals that had ne'er the fortune 200
To keep on their own hats, but let horns wear 'em;
Nine coaches waiting – hurry, hurry, hurry –

CASTIZA
Ay, to the devil!

VINDICE
[Aside] Ay, to the devil. – To the duke by my faith!

GRATIANA
Ay, to the duke. Daughter you'd scorn to think o' the 205
devil an you were there once.

VINDICE
[Aside] True, for most there are as proud as he for his heart,
i' faith –
Who'd sit at home in a neglected room

187 *forehead* See I. ii. 4 and n.
189–90 ed. (Start . . . presence / *Mother.* O . . . ravisht / *Cast.* I . . . honour / Q)
197–8 *one line in* Q
198 *quicken* enliven, with a play on the sense 'make pregnant'
199 *Musics* (Q) The plural form makes sense, signifying pieces of music performed.
        OED cites a usage in Sidney, *Arcadia* (OED sb 4).
200 *bare-headed vassals* Hats were not worn by men at court.
201 *horns* antlers used as hatracks, with a glance at the cuckold's horns (See I. ii. 107
        and n.)

Dealing her short-lived beauty to the pictures   210
That are as useless as old men, when those
Poorer in face and fortune than herself
Walk with a hundred acres on their backs –
Fair meadows cut into green foreparts – oh,
It was the greatest blessing ever happened to women   215
When farmers' sons agreed, and met again,
To wash their hands and come up gentlemen;
The commonwealth has flourished ever since.
Lands that were mete by the rod – that labour's spared –
Tailors ride down and measure 'em by the yard.   220
Fair trees, those comely foretops of the field,
Are cut to maintain head-tires: much untold.
All thrives but Chastity, she lies a-cold.
Nay shall I come nearer to you: mark but this:
Why are there so few honest women but because 'tis the   225
poorer profession? That's accounted best that's best
followed, least in trade, least in fashion, and that's not
honesty, believe it; and do but note the low and dejected
price of it:
'Lose but a pearl, we search and cannot brook it;   230
But that once gone, who is so mad to look it?'
GRATIANA
Troth he says true.
CASTIZA   False! I defy you both:
I have endured you with an ear of fire,
Your tongues have struck hot irons on my face;
Mother, come from that poisonous woman there.   235

---

211 *useless* i.e., in terms of sensuous pleasure
213 i.e. their clothes cost as much as a hundred acres of land
214 *green foreparts* (i) the park in front of a manor-house, (ii) an ornamental part of
   a woman's dress, covering the breast
217 i.e., exchange their honest working lives as farmers for the foppish existence of
   gentlemen in town and at court
219–20 The destruction of tradition is ironically imaged in the different scales of
   measurement used by the farming gentry and merchant tailors. Even when the
   city tailor buys a manor in the country he retains the acquisitive attitudes of the
   shopkeeper instead of adopting the values of conservation and continuity
   associated with keeping a country estate.
219 *mete by the rod* measured in rods (the customary measuring unit for land)
220 *yard* the unit of measure for cloth, the cloth-yard
221 *foretops* front lock of hair arranged ornamentally
222 *head-tires* head-dresses
228 *low* ed. (loue Q)
230 *brook it* bear its loss

GRATIANA
  Where?
CASTIZA
  Do you not see her? She's too inward then:
  Slave perish in thy office; you heavens please
  Henceforth to make the mother a disease
  Which first begins with me; yet I've outgone you.   *Exit*   240
VINDICE
  [*Aside*] Oh angels clap your wings upon the skies
  And give this virgin crystal plaudities!
GRATIANA
  Peevish, coy, foolish! But return this answer:
  My lord shall be most welcome when his pleasure
  Conducts him this way; I will sway mine own: 245
  Women with women can work best alone.   *Exit*
VINDICE
  Indeed I'll tell him so.
  Oh more uncivil, more unnatural
  Than those base-titled creatures that look downward,
  Why does not heaven turn black or with a frown   250
  Undo the world? Why does not earth start up
  And strike the sins that tread upon it? Oh,
  Were't not for gold and women there would be no
     damnation,
  Hell would look like a lord's great kitchen without fire
     in't;
  But 'twas decreed before the world began   255
  That they should be the hooks to catch at man.   *Exit*

[Act II, Scene ii]

Enter LUSSURIOSO *with* HIPPOLITO (VINDICE'S *brother*)

LUSSURIOSO
  I much applaud
  Thy judgement, thou art well read in a fellow,
  And 'tis the deepest art to study man.
  I know this which I never learned in schools,
  The world's divided into knaves and fools.   5
HIPPOLITO
  [*Aside*] Knave in your face my lord – behind your back!
LUSSURIOSO
  And I much thank thee that thou hast preferred

253–4 *verse in* Q; *as prose*, Foakes

A fellow of discourse, well mingled,
And whose brain time hath seasoned.
HIPPOLITO   True my lord,
  We shall find season once I hope. – [*Aside*] Oh villain,   10
  To make such an unnatural slave of me! – But –

           [*Enter* VINDICE *disguised*]

LUSSURIOSO
  Mass here he comes.
HIPPOLITO [*Aside*]   And now shall I
  Have free leave to depart.
LUSSURIOSO   Your absence – leave us.
HIPPOLITO
  [*Aside*] Are not my thoughts true? I must remove;
  But brother you may stay.   15
  Heart, we are both made bawds a new found way!   *Exit*
LUSSURIOSO
  Now, we're an even number: a third man's dangerous,
  Especially her brother. Say, be free,
  Have I a pleasure toward?
VINDICE   Oh my lord.
LUSSURIOSO
  Ravish me in thine answer: art thou rare,   20
  Hast thou beguiled her of salvation
  And rubbed hell o'er with honey? Is she a woman?
VINDICE
  In all but in desire.
LUSSURIOSO   Then she's in nothing –
  I bate in courage now.
VINDICE   The word I brought
  Might well have made indifferent honest naught;   25
  A right good woman in these days is changed
  Into white money with less labour far –
  Many a maid has turned to Mahomet
  With easier working. I durst undertake,
  Upon the pawn and forfeit of my life   30
  With half those words to flat a Puritan's wife,
  But she is close and good; yet 'tis a doubt
  By this time – oh the mother, the mother!

23–4 ed. (In . . . desire / Then . . . now / The . . . brought / Q)
25 *indifferent honest naught* a person of average virtue wicked
27 *white* silver
28–9 many a virgin has been converted with less difficulty to the worship of
    Mahomet
32–3 *one line in* Q

LUSSURIOSO
    I never thought their sex had been a wonder
    Until this minute: what fruit from the mother?   35
VINDICE
    [*Aside*] Now must I blister my soul, be forsworn,
    Or shame the woman that received me first.
    I will be true; thou liv'st not to proclaim;
    Spoke to a dying man shame has no shame.
    My lord.
LUSSURIOSO   Who's that?
VINDICE   Here's none but I my lord.   40
LUSSURIOSO
    What would thy haste utter?
VINDICE   Comfort.
LUSSURIOSO   Welcome.
VINDICE
    The maid being dull, having no mind to travel
    Into unknown lands, what did me I straight
    But set spurs to the mother; golden spurs
    Will put her to a false gallop in a trice.   45
LUSSURIOSO
    Is't possible that in this
    The mother should be damned before the daughter?
VINDICE
    Oh that's good manners my lord: the mother for her age
    must go foremost you know.
LUSSURIOSO
    Thou'st spoke that true! But where comes in this
    comfort?   50
VINDICE
    In a fine place my lord. The unnatural mother
    Did with her tongue so hard beset her honour
    That the poor fool was struck to silent wonder;
    Yet still the maid like an unlighted taper
    Was cold and chaste, save that her mother's breath   55
    Did blow fire on her cheeks. The girl departed
    But the good ancient madam, half mad, threw me
    These promising words which I took deeply note of:
    'My lord shall be most welcome,' –
LUSSURIOSO   Faith I thank her!

---

43 *did me I* did I do
48–9 *prose in* Q
56 *blow . . . cheeks* i.e., made her blush
    cheeks ed. (checkes Q)

VINDICE
'When his pleasure conducts him this way' –   60
LUSSURIOSO
That shall be soon i' faith!
VINDICE   'I will sway mine own' –
LUSSURIOSO
She does the wiser, I commend her for't.
VINDICE
'Women with women can work best alone.'
LUSSURIOSO
By this light and so they can; give 'em their due, men are
not comparable to 'em.   65
VINDICE
No that's true, for you shall have one woman knit more in a
hour than any man can ravel again in seven and twenty
year.
LUSSURIOSO
Now my desires are happy, I'll make 'em freemen now.
Thou art a precious fellow, faith I love thee,   70
Be wise and make it thy revenue: beg, leg!
What office couldst thou be ambitious for?
VINDICE
Office my lord! Marry if I might have my wish I would
have one that was never begged yet.
LUSSURIOSO
Nay then thou canst have none.   75
VINDICE
Yes my lord, I could pick out another office yet, nay and
keep a horse and drab upon it.
LUSSURIOSO
Prithee good bluntness tell me –
VINDICE
Why I would desire but this my lord: to have all the fees

64–5 *prose in* Q
68 *ravel* unravel
71 *beg, leg* beg and bow in a servile manner
77 *drab* mistress
79 *fees* Ironically proposing a new tax on love-making. There was enough room
   between the hangings and the wall for people to conceal themselves – thus
   Polonius hides behind the arras in Hamlet's mother's bedchamber and is killed
   there by Hamlet.

behind the arras, and all the farthingales that fall plump   80
about twelve o'clock at night upon the rushes.

LUSSURIOSO

Thou'rt a mad apprehensive knave: dost think to make any
great purchase of that?

VINDICE

Oh 'tis an unknown thing my lord; I wonder 't'as been
missed so long!   85

LUSSURIOSO

Well this night I'll visit her, and 'tis till then
A year in my desires. Farewell, attend,
Trust me with thy preferment.   *Exit*

VINDICE   My loved lord. –
Oh shall I kill him o' the wrong-side now? No,
Sword thou wast never a back-biter yet.   90
I'll pierce him to his face, he shall die looking upon me;
Thy veins are swelled with lust, this shall unfill 'em:
Great men were gods if beggars could not kill 'em.
Forgive me heaven to call my mother wicked,
Oh lessen not my days upon the earth!   95
I cannot honour her; by this I fear me
Her tongue has turned my sister into use.
I was a villain not to be forsworn
To this our lecherous hope, the duke's son;
For lawyers, merchants, some divines and all,   100
Count beneficial perjury a sin small.
It shall go hard yet but I'll guard her honour
And keep the ports sure.

Enter HIPPOLITO

HIPPOLITO

Brother how goes the world? I would know news
Of you, but I have news to tell you.   105

80 *farthingales* hooped petticoats
   plump (adv) with an abrupt fall (OED adv 2), implying that they are dropped
   with impatient haste
81 *rushes* These were strewn on the floors of houses and theatre stages.
82 *mad apprehensive* witty, crazy
89 Perhaps recalling *Hamlet* III. iii. 73: 'Now might I do it pat'.
95 Alluding to Exodus 20:12.
97 *use* the gold of virginity sold, made current
101 *beneficial perjury* Apparently alluding to equivocation. Father Garnet, a Jesuit,
   implicated in the Gunpowder Plot, claimed the right to make ambiguous
   answers under interrogation in order not to incriminate himself. This made the
   topic one of current scandulous interest. See *Macbeth* II. iii. 8–11.
104–5 ed. (Brother . . . you / But . . . you / Q)

VINDICE
  What, in the name of knavery?
HIPPOLITO   Knavery faith:
  This vicious old duke's worthily abused,
  The pen of his bastard writes him cuckold!
VINDICE
  His bastard?
HIPPOLITO   Pray believe it; he and the duchess
  By night meet in their linen, they have been seen   110
  By stair-foot pandars.
VINDICE   Oh sin foul and deep,
  Great faults are winked at when the duke's asleep.
  See, see, here comes the Spurio –

                [*Enter* SPURIO *with two men*]

HIPPOLITO   Monstrous luxur!
VINDICE
  Unbraced: two of his valiant bawds with him.
  Oh there's a wicked whisper; hell is in his ear.   115
  Stay, let's observe his passage. –   [*They retire*]
SPURIO
  Oh but are you sure on't?
SERVANT
  My lord most sure on't, for 'twas spoke by one
  That is most inward with the duke's son's lust;
  That he intends within this hour to steal   120
  Unto Hippolito's sister, whose chaste life
  The mother has corrupted for his use.
SPURIO
  Sweet word, sweet occasion, faith then brother
  I'll disinherit you in as short time
  As I was when I was begot in haste,   125
  I'll damn you at your pleasure: precious deed!
  After your lust oh 'twill be fine to bleed!
  Come let our passing out be soft and wary.
                          Exeunt [SPURIO *and two men*]
VINDICE
  Mark, there, there, that step! Now to the duchess;
  This their second meeting writes the duke cuckold   130
  With new additions, his horns newly revived;

---

114 *Unbraced* not fully or properly dressed
131 *addition* In the sense (ironic) of honours: his coat of arms is crested with
    cuckold's horns.

Night, thou that look'st like funeral herald's fees
Torn down betimes i' the morning, thou hang'st fitly
To grace those sins that have no grace at all.
Now 'tis full sea abed over the world,	135
There's juggling of all sides. Some that were maids
E'en at sunset are now perhaps i' the toll-book;
This woman in immodest thin apparel
Lets in her friend by water, here a dame
Cunning, nails leather hinges to a door	140
To avoid proclamation.
Now cuckolds are a-coining, apace, apace, apace, apace!
And careful sisters spin that thread i' the night
That does maintain them and their bawds i' the day.

HIPPOLITO
You flow well brother.
VINDICE	Puh I'm shallow yet,	145
Too sparing and too modest; shall I tell thee,
If every trick were told that's dealt by night
There are few here that would not blush outright.

HIPPOLITO
I am of that belief too.
VINDICE	Who's this comes?

[*Enter* LUSSURIOSO]

The duke's son up so late! Brother fall back	150
And you shall learn some mischief. – My good lord.

---

132 *funeral herald's fees* Collins supposes *fees* = phease, hangings of black cloth put
up for a funeral. Foakes suggests the additional allusion to the high fees charged
by heralds for the display of escutcheons and other trappings exhibiting the
dead person's noble lineage.
135 *full sea* high tide. See other water images at I. iii. 52, 91–2.
136 *juggling* deception
137 *toll-book* Strictly speaking, the toll-book listed horses for sale at a fair. Here it is
used ironically.
140 *leather hinges* i.e., to reduce noise and evade detection. Compare *The
Malcontent* I. vii. 38–41, *The Atheist's Tragedy* I. iv. 146.
141 *proclamation* public exposure
142 *a-coining* being coined. For the metaphor of coining for begetting see *Measure
for Measure* II. iv. 45–6.
143 *sisters* OED cites a 1550 usage, 'sisters of the Bank' (i.e. Bankside) = prostitutes.
spin that thread like silk worms, their own bodies are a luxurious source of profit
150 *The duke's* ed. (*Vind.* The Dukes Q) This is the first line of the page on D4v in
Q, but the catchword on D4 has no speech heading for Vindice. Perhaps Q
caught the SH from the final line on D4: '*Vind.* Whose this comes'. I assume the
catchword is correct.

LUSSURIOSO
  Piato, why the man I wished for, come,
  I do embrace this season for the fittest
  To taste of that young lady.
VINDICE [*Aside*]   Heart and hell!
HIPPOLITO
  [*Aside*] Damned villain!   155
VINDICE
  [*Aside*] I ha' no way now to cross it, but to kill him.
LUSSURIOSO
  Come, only thou and I.
VINDICE   My lord, my lord.
LUSSURIOSO
  Why dost thou start us?
VINDICE
  I'd almost forgot – the bastard!
LUSSURIOSO   What of him?
VINDICE
  This night, this hour – this minute, now –   160
LUSSURIOSO
  What? What?
VINDICE   Shadows the duchess –
LUSSURIOSO   Horrible word.
VINDICE
  And like strong poison eats
  Into the duke your father's forehead.
LUSSURIOSO   Oh!
VINDICE
  He makes horn royal.
LUSSURIOSO   Most ignoble slave!
VINDICE
  This is the fruit of two beds.
LUSSURIOSO   I am mad.   165
VINDICE
  That passage he trod warily.
LUSSURIOSO   He did!
VINDICE
  And hushed his villains every step he took.

---

152 *Piato* Florio defines the Italian as (i) hidden, (ii) plated, (iii) pleader. The
   connotation of deception seems appropriate.
164 *horn royal* a royal cuckold; but perhaps 'royal' carries the sense 'riotously,
   extremely' as in the phrase 'sport royal' (*Twelfth Night* II. iii. 172). There may
   be a recollection of the term *horn-mad* = enraged, or of *royal antlers*, the branch
   of a stag's horns above the brow-antler (OED).

LUSSURIOSO

His villains! I'll confound them.

VINDICE

Take 'em finely, finely now.

LUSSURIOSO

The duchess' chamber door shall not control me.   170

Exeunt [LUSSURIOSO *and* VINDICE]

HIPPOLITO

Good, happy, swift, there's gunpowder i' the Court,
Wildfire at midnight! In this heedless fury
He may show violence to cross himself:
I'll follow the event.   *Exit*

[Act II, Scene iii]

[*The* DUKE *and* DUCHESS *discovered in bed.*] *Enter again*
[LUSSURIOSO *and* VINDICE *disguised*]

LUSSURIOSO

Where is that villain?

VINDICE

Softly my lord and you may take 'em twisted.

LUSSURIOSO

I care not how!

VINDICE   Oh 'twill be glorious,
To kill 'em doubled, when they're heaped – be soft my lord.

LUSSURIOSO

Away! My spleen is not so lazy – thus, and thus,   5
I'll shake their eyelids ope and with my sword
Shut 'em again for ever: villain! Strumpet!

[*They approach the bed*]

170 *control* prevent
173 i.e., he may become violent and so thwart his own aims
  0 sd The scene may have been played as a night scene, the characters carrying
    lighted torches, as stage convention dictated. In other plays of the time sd's have
    the wording '*bed put forth*'. The bed, with drawn curtains concealing the
    occupants, could be pushed on stage through the doors in the tiring-house wall.
    In *Romeo & Juliet*, after the heroine swallows a potion there is the sd '*She falls
    upon her bed within the curtains*' (IV. iii), where a bed may have been 'put forth'
    or where a curtain across an opening in the tiring-house façade, suggesting a
    curtained four-poster bed, was used. It is important in the present scene that
    both occupants be discovered as if in bed, as the dialogue shows.
2–4 Compare *Hamlet* III. iii. 88–95.

DUKE
  You upper guard defend us!
DUCHESS   Treason, treason!
DUKE
  Oh take me not in sleep,
  I have great sins, I must have days,   10
  Nay months dear son, with penitential heaves,
  To lift 'em out and not to die unclear;
  Oh thou wilt kill me both in heaven and here.
LUSSURIOSO
  I am amazed to death.
DUKE   Nay villain, traitor,
  Worse than the foulest epithet, now I'll grip thee   15
  E'en with the nerves of wrath, and throw thy head
  Amongst the lawyers. Guard!

  Enter nobles and sons [AMBITIOSO *and* SUPERVACUO *with*
                    HIPPOLITO]

1 NOBLE
  How comes the quiet of your Grace disturbed?
DUKE
  This boy that should be myself after me
  Would be myself before me, and in heat   20
  Of that ambition bloodily rushed in
  Intending to depose me in my bed.
2 NOBLE
  Duty and natural loyalty forfend!
DUCHESS
  He called his father villain and me strumpet,
  A word that I abhor to 'file my lips with.   25
AMBITIOSO
  That was not so well done brother!
LUSSURIOSO   I am abused:
  I know there's no excuse can do me good.
VINDICE
  [*Aside to* HIPPOLITO] 'Tis now good policy to be from sight;
  His vicious purpose to our sister's honour
  Is crossed beyond our thought.
HIPPOLITO   You little dreamed   30
  His father slept here?
VINDICE   Oh 'twas far beyond me.

9–11 ed. (Oh . . . daies / Nay . . . heaues / Q)
25 *'file* defile
26–7 ed. (I am . . . good / Q)
30–1 ed. (Is . . . thought / You . . . here / Oh . . . me / Q)

But since it fell so – without frightful word –
Would he had killed him, 'twould have eased our swords.
                    [*Exeunt* VINDICE *and* HIPPOLITO *stealthily*]

DUKE
Be comforted our duchess, he shall die.

LUSSURIOSO
Where's this slave-pandar now? Out of mine eye,   35
Guilty of this abuse.

                    Enter SPURIO *with his villains*

SPURIO
Y'are villains, fablers,
You have knaves' chins and harlots' tongues, you lie,
And I will damn you with one meal a day!

1 SERVANT
Oh good my lord!

SPURIO   'Sblood you shall never sup.   40

2 SERVANT
Oh I beseech you sir!

SPURIO   To let my sword
Catch cold so long and miss him!

1 SERVANT   Troth my lord,
'Twas his intent to meet there.

SPURIO   Heart he's yonder!
Ha? What news here? Is the day out o' the socket,
That it is noon at midnight, the Court up?   45
How comes the guard so saucy with his elbows?

LUSSURIOSO
The bastard here?
Nay then the truth of my intent shall out –
My lord and father, hear me.

DUKE   Bear him hence.

LUSSURIOSO
I can with loyalty excuse –   50

---

33 *eased . . . swords* saved us the trouble
33 sd ed. (*dissemble a flight* Q)
41–3 ed. (O . . . sir/To . . . him/Troth . . . there/Q)
44 *day . . . socket* Compare I. iv. 26–8 'torchlight made an artificial noon'. The
regular place of the sun is compared to a torch fixed in its wall-socket. The
blaze of many torches (brought in by the assembling company) makes the scene
as bright as day, and furthermore, with such unnatural crimes, ominous
perturbations in the heavens might well be expected (see *Macbeth* II. i. 4–5 and
II. iv. 4–11). There may also be a submerged link with the skull–eye–eye-
socket–diamond–collet images earlier.

DUKE
  Excuse? To prison with the villain:
  Death shall not long lag after him.
SPURIO
  [*Aside*] Good i' faith, then 'tis not much amiss.
LUSSURIOSO
  Brothers my best release lies on your tongues,
  I pray persuade for me.
AMBITIOSO   It is our duties: 55
  Make yourself sure of us.
SUPERVACUO   We'll sweat in pleading.
LUSSURIOSO
  And I may live to thank you.
                        Exeunt [LUSSURIOSO *and guards*]
AMBITIOSO [*Aside*]   No, thy death
  Shall thank me better.
SPURIO [*Aside*]   He's gone – I'll after him,
  And know his trespass, seem to bear a part
  In all his ills – but with a Puritan heart.   *Exit*   60
AMBITIOSO
  Now brother let our hate and love be woven
  So subtly together that in speaking
  One word for his life, we may make three for his death;
  The craftiest pleader gets most gold for breath.
SUPERVACUO
  Set on, I'll not be far behind you brother.   65
DUKE
  Is't possible a son should
  Be disobedient as far as the sword?
  It is the highest, he can go no farther.
AMBITIOSO
  My gracious lord take pity.
DUKE   Pity, boys?
AMBITIOSO
  Nay we'd be loth to move your grace too much: 70
  We know the trespass is unpardonable,
  Black, wicked and unnatural.
SUPERVACUO
  In a son, oh monstrous!
AMBITIOSO   Yet my lord

55–8 ed.   (It . . . us / Weele . . . pleading / And . . . you / No . . . better / Hee's . . .
   him / Q)
60 *Puritan* hypocritical
62–3 ed. (So . . . life / We . . . death / Q)
66–8 *prose in* Q

A duke's soft hand strokes the rough head of law
And makes it lie smooth.

DUKE   But my hand shall ne'er do't.   75

AMBITIOSO
That as you please my lord.

SUPERVACUO   We must needs confess
Some father would have entered into hate
So deadly-pointed, that before his eyes
He would ha' seen the execution sound
Without corrupted favour.

AMBITIOSO   But my lord,   80
Your Grace may live the wonder of all times
In pard'ning that offence which never yet
Had face to beg a pardon.

DUKE   Honey how's this?

AMBITIOSO
Forgive him good my lord, he's your own son,
And – I must needs say – 'twas the vilelier done.   85

SUPERVACUO
He's the next heir; yet this true reason gathers;
None can possess that dispossess their fathers.
Be merciful –

DUKE [*Aside*]   Here's no stepmother's wit:
I'll try 'em both upon their love and hate.

AMBITIOSO
Be merciful – although –

DUKE   You have prevailed,   90
My wrath like flaming wax hath spent itself,
I know 'twas but some peevish moon in him:
Go, let him be released.

SUPERVACUO [*Aside*]   'Sfoot how now brother?

AMBITIOSO
Your Grace doth please to speak beside your spleen;
I would it were so happy.

DUKE   Why, go release him.   95

SUPERVACUO
Oh my good lord I know the fault's too weighty
And full of general loathing, too inhuman,
Rather by all men's voices worthy death.

---

78 *deadly-pointed* i.e., fatally dangerous (as of a weapon)
79 *sound* i.e., secure. Compare III. iv. 26 (Nicoll).
92 *moon* fit of lunacy
92–3 ed. (I know . . . releas'd Q)

DUKE
  'Tis true too.
  Here then receive this signet; doom shall pass.   100
  Direct it to the judges. He shall die
  Ere many days – make haste.
AMBITIOSO   All speed that may be.
  We could have wished his burden not so sore,
  We knew your Grace did but delay before.
            Exeunt [AMBITIOSO *and* SUPERVACUO]
DUKE
  Here's envy with a poor thin cover o'er it,   105
  Like scarlet hid in lawn, easily spied through;
  This their ambition by the mother's side
  Is dangerous and for safety must be purged.
  I will prevent their envies, sure it was
  But some mistaken fury in our son   110
  Which these aspiring boys would climb upon;
  He shall be released suddenly.

            Enter Nobles

1 NOBLE
  Good morning to your Grace.
DUKE   Welcome my lords.
                    [*The nobles kneel*]
2 NOBLE
  Our knees shall take away the office of our feet for ever,
  Unless your Grace bestow a father's eye   115
  Upon the clouded fortunes of your son,
  And in compassionate virtue grant him that
  Which makes e'en mean men happy: liberty.
DUKE
  [*Aside*] How seriously their loves and honours woo
  For that which I am about to pray them do. –   120
  Rise my lords, your knees sign his release:
  We freely pardon him.
1 NOBLE
  We owe your Grace much thanks, and he much duty.
                  Exeunt [*nobles*]
DUKE
  It well becomes that judge to nod at crimes

99–102 ed. (Tis . . . passe / Direct . . . dye / Ere . . . hast / Q)
100 *signet* The word was used for King James I's own seal (OED).
105 *o'er it* ed. (or't Q)
106 Scarlet cloth would show through the fine linen worn over it
121 *Rise my lords* ed. (Which, rise my lords Q)

That does commit greater himself and lives.   125
I may forgive a disobedient error
That expect pardon for adultery,
And in my old days am a youth in lust.
Many a beauty have I turned to poison
In the denial, covetous of all;   130
Age hot, is like a monster to be seen:
My hairs are white and yet my sins are green.   [*Exit*]

Act III [Scene i]

Enter AMBITIOSO *and* SUPERVACUO

SUPERVACUO
Brother let my opinion sway you once;
I speak it for the best to have him die
Surest and soonest; if the signet come
Unto the judge's hands, why then his doom
Will be deferred till sittings and court-days,   5
Juries and further; faiths are bought and sold,
Oaths in these days are but the skin of gold.
AMBITIOSO
In troth 'tis true too.
SUPERVACUO   Then let's set by the judges
And fall to the officers; 'tis but mistaking
The duke our father's meaning, and where he named   10
'Ere many days' 'tis but forgetting that
And have him die i' the morning.
AMBITIOSO   Excellent!
Then am I heir – duke in a minute!
SUPERVACUO [*Aside*]   Nay,
And he were once puffed out, here is a pin
Should quickly prick your bladder.
AMBITIOSO   Blest occasion!   15
He being packed we'll have some trick and wile
To wind our younger brother out of prison
That lies in for the rape; the lady's dead
And people's thoughts will soon be burièd.

129–30 i.e., I have poisoned many a beauty who denied my suit – I desire every one
    of them.
 14 *puffed out* i.e., killed, blown out like a candle flame
 15 *Blest* ed. (Blast Q)
 16 *packed* got rid of

SUPERVACUO
 We may with safety do't and live and feed: 20
 The duchess' sons are too proud to bleed.
AMBITIOSO
 We are i' faith to say true. Come let's not linger –
 I'll to the officers, go you before
 And set an edge upon the executioner.
SUPERVACUO
 Let me alone to grind him.   *Exit*
AMBITIOSO   Meet; farewell.   25
 I am next now, I rise just in that place
 Where thou'rt cut off – upon thy neck kind brother;
 The falling of one head lifts up another.   *Exit*

[Act III, Scene ii]

Enter with the nobles LUSSURIOSO *from prison*

LUSSURIOSO
 My lords
 I am so much indebted to your loves
 For this, oh this delivery.
1 NOBLE   But our duties
 My lord unto the hopes that grow in you.
LUSSURIOSO
 If e'er I live to be myself I'll thank you.   5
 Oh liberty thou sweet and heavenly dame!
 But hell, for prison, is too mild a name! *Exeunt*

[Act III, Scene iii]

Enter AMBITIOSO *and* SUPERVACUO *with officers*

AMBITIOSO
 Officers, here's the duke's signet, your firm warrant,
 Brings the command of present death along with it
 Unto our brother the duke's son; we are sorry

---

24 *set . . . executioner* sharpen the axe. There is a subsidiary sense: urge the officer
 to put him quickly to death.

1–2 ed. (My . . . loves / Q)

3–5 ed. (For . . . delivery / But . . . you / Q)

1 The situation is reminiscent of *Richard III* I. iv., where the two murderers bring
 Brackenbury the warrant to deliver Clarence, Richard's brother, to them.

That we are so unnaturally employed
In such an unkind office, fitter far   5
For enemies than brothers.

SUPERVACUO   But you know
The duke's command must be obeyed.

1 OFFICER
It must and shall my lord – this morning then,
So suddenly?

AMBITIOSO   Ay alas poor good soul,
He must breakfast betimes, the executioner   10
Stands ready to put forth his cowardly valour.

2 OFFICER
Already?

SUPERVACUO
Already i' faith; oh sir destruction hies,
And that is least impudent, soonest dies.

1 OFFICER
Troth you say true my lord; we take our leaves.   15
Our office shall be sound, we'll not delay
The third part of a minute.

AMBITIOSO   Therein you show
Yourselves good men and upright officers;
Pray let him die as private as he may,
Do him that favour, for the gaping people   20
Will but trouble him at his prayers
And make him curse and swear and so die black.
Will you be so far kind?

1 OFFICER   It shall be done my lord.

AMBITIOSO
Why we do thank you; if we live to be,
You shall have a better office.

2 OFFICER   Your good lordship.   25

SUPERVACUO
Commend us to the scaffold in our tears.

1 OFFICER
We'll weep and do your commendations.   *Exeunt [officers]*

AMBITIOSO
Fine fools in office!

SUPERVACUO   Things fall out so fit!

AMBITIOSO
So happily! Come brother ere next clock
His head will be made serve a bigger block.   *Exeunt*   30

9 *poor good soul* ed. (poor-good-soul Q)
16 *sound* reliably, properly carried out
30 *block* (i) execution block, (ii) hat-size

[Act III, Scene iv]

Enter [YOUNGER SON *and his prison* KEEPER]

YOUNGER SON
  Keeper.
KEEPER   My lord.
YOUNGER SON   No news lately from our brothers?
  Are they unmindful of us?
KEEPER
  My lord a messenger came newly in
  And brought this from 'em.   [*He gives him a letter*]
YOUNGER SON   Nothing but paper comforts?
  I looked for my delivery before this;   5
  Had they been worth their oaths – prithee be from us;
                              [*Exit* KEEPER]
  Now, what say you forsooth? Speak out I pray:
                        [*He reads out the*] *letter*
  'Brother be of good cheer' –
  'Slud it begins like a whore with good cheer!
  'Thou shalt not be long a prisoner' –   10
  Not five and thirty year like a bankrupt, I think so!
  'We have thought upon a device to get thee out by a trick' –
  By a trick! Pox o' your trick and it be so long a playing.
  'And so rest comforted, be merry and expect it suddenly' –
  Be merry, hang merry, draw and quarter merry, I'll be mad!   15
  Is't not strange that a man should lie in a whole month for a
  woman? Well, we shall see how sudden our brothers will be
  in their promise, I must expect still a trick: I shall not be
  long a prisoner. How now, what news?

                  [*Enter* KEEPER]

KEEPER
  Bad news my lord, I am discharged of you.   20
YOUNGER SON
  Slave, call'st thou that bad news! I thank you brothers.
KEEPER
  My lord 'twill prove so; here come the officers
  Into whose hands I must commit you.   [*Exit* KEEPER]

  3–4 ed. (My . . . 'em / Nothing . . . comforts / Q)
  15 *hang . . . quarter* Hanging, disembowelling and cutting in quarters was the
    punishment for treason in England at the time.
    Perhaps a sd should be added: *Tears up the letter* (see line 57 below).
  16 *lie in* the usual term for a woman's confinement at childbirth

YOUNGER SON
  Ha, officers? What, why?

                    [*Enter* OFFICERS]

1 OFFICER
  You must pardon us my lord,   25
  Our office must be sound, here is our warrant,
  The signet from the duke; you must straight suffer.
YOUNGER SON
  Suffer? I'll suffer you to be gone, I'll suffer you
  To come no more – what would you have me suffer?
2 OFFICER
  My lord those words were better changed to prayers,   30
  The time's but brief with you; prepare to die.
YOUNGER SON
  Sure 'tis not so.
3 OFFICER   It is too true my lord.
YOUNGER SON
  I tell you 'tis not, for the duke my father
  Deferred me till next sitting, and I look
  E'en every minute, threescore times an hour   35
  For a release, a trick, wrought by my brothers.
1 OFFICER
  A trick my lord? If you expect such comfort
  Your hope's as fruitless as a barren woman:
  Your brothers were the unhappy messengers
  That brought this powerful token for your death.   40
YOUNGER SON
  My brothers! No, no!
2 OFFICER   'Tis most true my lord.
YOUNGER SON
  My brothers to bring a warrant for my death:
  How strange this shows!
3 OFFICER   There's no delaying time.
YOUNGER SON
  Desire 'em hither, call 'em up, my brothers –
  They shall deny it to your faces!
1 OFFICER   My lord,   45
  They're far enough by this, at least at Court,
  And this most strict command they left behind 'em
  When grief swum in their eyes: they showed like brothers,

26 *sound* See III. iii. 16 and n.
34 *sitting* session of the law-courts

Brim-full of heavy sorrow; but the duke
Must have his pleasure.
YOUNGER SON   His pleasure?   50
1 OFFICER
These were their last words which my memory bears:
'Commend us to the scaffold in our tears'.
YOUNGER SON
Pox dry their tears: what should I do with tears?
I hate 'em worse than any citizen's son
Can hate salt water. Here came a letter now,   55
New bleeding from their pens, scarce stinted yet –
Would I'd been torn in pieces when I tore it –
Look you officious whoresons, words of comfort:
'Not long a prisoner'.
1 OFFICER
It says true in that sir, for you must suffer presently.   60
YOUNGER SON
A villainous Duns upon the letter: knavish exposition!
Look you then here sir: 'We'll get thee out by a trick'
says he.
2 OFFICER
That may hold too sir, for you know a trick is commonly
four cards, which was meant by us four officers.   65
YOUNGER SON
Worse and worse dealing.
1 OFFICER   The hour beckons us,
The headsman waits: lift up your eyes to heaven.
YOUNGER SON
I thank you faith, good pretty wholesome counsel!
I should look up to heaven as you said

---

52 *italic in* Q

53–4 The Younger Son introduces a strong element of farce into the melodramatic
    atmosphere, strongly indebted as it is here to *Richard III*, where the reciprocal
    effects of melodrama and farce are vividly apparent. Sympathetic theatrical
    interpretation of *The Revenger's Tragedy* confounds hostile critics of the
    farcical element in the play.

54–5 *worse . . . water* Citizens, as mere land-lubbers, find the sea and voyages by
    sea frightening, although the city profits from being a port and invests in
    shipping. Possibly there is an allusion (as Foakes suggests) to press-gangs
    enforcing civilians to serve in the navy.

61 *Duns* The medieval scholastic philosopher Duns Scotus, known for his hair-
    splitting distinctions, is here invoked by the exasperated Younger Son on
    hearing this sophistical interpretation of 'not long'. *Duns* came to be a common
    proverbial term for fool, surviving in the modern word *dunce*.

Whilst he behind me cozens me of my head!   70
Ay, that's the trick.
3 OFFICER   You delay too long my lord.
YOUNGER SON
Stay good authority's bastards: since I must
Through brothers' perjury die, oh let me venom
Their souls with curses.
1 OFFICER   Come 'tis no time to curse.
YOUNGER SON
Must I bleed then without respect of sign? Well –   75
My fault was sweet sport which the world approves;
I die for that which every woman loves.   *Exeunt*

[Act III, Scene v]

Enter VINDICE [*disguised*] *with* HIPPOLITO *his brother*

VINDICE
Oh sweet, delectable, rare, happy, ravishing!
HIPPOLITO
Why what's the matter brother?
VINDICE   Oh 'tis able
To make a man spring up and knock his forehead
Against yon silver ceiling.
HIPPOLITO   Prithee tell me
Why may not I partake with you? You vowed once   5
To give me share to every tragic thought.
VINDICE
By th' Mass I think I did too:
Then I'll divide it to thee. The old duke,
Thinking my outward shape and inward heart
Are cut out of one piece – for he that prates his secrets,   10
His heart stands o' the outside – hires me by price
To greet him with a lady
In some fit place veiled from the eyes o' the Court,
Some darkened blushless angle that is guilty
Of his forefathers' lusts, and great folks' riots;   15

75 G. B. Harrison remarks that medical bleeding had to be done under favourable
   astrological conditions.

2–3 ed. (Why . . . brother / O . . . for-head / Q)

4 *silver ceiling* the sky (with punning allusions to the real sky above the open-air
   Globe Theatre where the play was performed, and to the canopy over the stage
   which was painted to suggest the heavens)

14 *guilty* in the sense of having witnessed guilty acts

To which I easily, to maintain my shape,
Consented, and did wish his impudent Grace
To meet her here in this unsunned lodge
Wherein 'tis night at noon, and here the rather
Because unto the torturing of his soul   20
The bastard and the duchess have appointed
Their meeting too in this luxurious circle –
Which most afflicting sight will kill his eyes
Before we kill the rest of him.

HIPPOLITO
'Twill i' faith, most dreadfully digested.   25
I see not how you could have missed me brother.

VINDICE
True, but the violence of my joy forgot it.

HIPPOLITO
Ay; but where's that lady now?

VINDICE   Oh at that word
I'm lost again, you cannot find me yet,
I'm in a throng of happy apprehensions!   30
He's suited for a lady: I have took care
For a delicious lip, a sparkling eye:
You shall be witness brother,
Be ready, stand with your hat off.   *Exit*

HIPPOLITO
Troth I wonder what lady it should be.   35
Yet 'tis no wonder now I think again
To have a lady stoop to a duke, that stoops unto his men:
'Tis common to be common, through the world,
And there's more private common shadowing vices
Than those who are known both by their names and prices.   40
'Tis part of my allegiance to stand bare
To the duke's concubine – and here she comes.

Enter VINDICE *with the skull of his love dressed up in tires*

VINDICE
Madam, his Grace will not be absent long.
Secret? Ne'er doubt us madam. 'Twill be worth
Three velvet gowns to your ladyship. Known?   45
Few ladies respect that; disgrace? A poor thin shell!
'Tis the best grace you have to do it well;
I'll save your hand that labour, I'll unmask you.
                    [VINDICE *reveals the skull*]

19 *night at noon* i.e., with an ominous implication
25 *digested* worked out, planned (OED lists a usage in chemistry, of 1607, meaning 'bring to maturity by the action of heat'.)

HIPPOLITO
Why brother, brother.
VINDICE
Art thou beguiled now? Tut a lady can   50
At such, all hid, beguile a wiser man.
Have I not fitted the old surfeiter
With a quaint piece of beauty? Age and bare bone
Are e'er allied in action. Here's an eye
Able to tempt a great man – to serve God;   55
A pretty hanging lip, that has forgot now to dissemble.
Methinks this mouth should make a swearer tremble,
A drunkard clasp his teeth, and not undo 'em
To suffer wet damnation to run through 'em.
Here's a cheek keeps her colour, let the wind go whistle: 60
Spout rain, we fear thee not, be hot or cold
All's one with us. And is not he absurd
Whose fortunes are upon their faces set,
That fear no other God but wind and wet?
HIPPOLITO
Brother y'ave spoke that right.   65
Is this the form that, living, shone so bright?
VINDICE
The very same.
And now methinks I could e'en chide myself
For doting on her beauty, though her death
Shall be revenged after no common action.   70
Does the silkworm expend her yellow labours
For thee? For thee does she undo herself?
Are lordships sold to maintain ladyships
For the poor benefit of a bewitching minute?
Why does yon fellow falsify highways   75

---

51 *all hid* the game of hide-and-seek, and a call in the game
58 *clasp* clench
59 *wet damnation* alcoholic drink (inducing the sin of drunkenness)
60–4 wind and rain are enemies to cosmetics. Recalling *King Lear* III. ii.1 and
   14–15; III. ii. in general and III. iv, especially III. iv. 101–9, and see *The
   Revenger's Tragedy* IV. ii.219–20.
71 *yellow* the colour of gold – hence, producing luxury, very costly – as well as the
   colour of the silkworm's cocoon
75 *fellow . . . highways* An obscure expression: *fellow* may stand for 'goodfellow',
   i.e., thief, and *falsify* may mean 'make unsafe', together giving the sense 'turn
   highwayman'. The idea may be that he tricks travellers into taking the wrong
   road in order to hold them up and rob them. One interpretation reads *highways*
   as the moral path of virtue which the fellow perverts and corrupts, *falsifies*.

And put his life between the judge's lips
To refine such a thing, keeps horse and men
To beat their valours for her?
Surely we're all mad people and they,
Whom we think are, are not: we mistake those.   80
'Tis we are mad in sense, they but in clothes.
HIPPOLITO
Faith and in clothes too we, give us our due.
VINDICE
Does every proud and self-affecting dame
Camphor her face for this, and grieve her maker
In sinful baths of milk, when many an infant starves   85
For her superfluous outside – all for this?
Who now bids twenty pound a night, prepares
Music, perfumes and sweetmeats? All are hushed,
Thou may'st lie chaste now! It were fine methinks
To have thee seen at revels, forgetful feasts   90
And unclean brothels; sure 'twould fright the sinner
And make him a good coward, put a reveller
Out of his antic amble
And cloy an epicure with empty dishes.
Here might a scornful and ambitious woman   95
Look through and through herself; see, ladies, with false
    forms
You deceive men but cannot deceive worms.
Now to my tragic business. Look you brother,
I have not fashioned this only for show
And useless property, no – it shall bear a part   100
E'en in it own revenge. This very skull,
Whose mistress the duke poisoned with this drug,
The mortal curse of the earth, shall be revenged
In the like strain and kiss his lips to death.
As much as the dumb thing can, he shall feel;   105
What fails in poison we'll supply in steel.

76 risk the death penalty
77 *refine* lavish finery and luxury upon
84 *Camphor* aromatic base for cosmetics
86 *superfluous outside* excessively pampered appearance or exterior
93 *antic amble* grotesque motion (Both words are perhaps remembering *Hamlet*,
    where the Prince adopts an 'antic disposition' and scorns the affectations of
    women, telling Ophelia 'You jig and amble' – see *Hamlet* I. v. 172, III. i. 144.)
100 *property* i.e., theatrical stage accessory (Presumably it could be the same skull
    used to represent Yorick's skull in the Globe's *Hamlet*.)
101 *it own* an Elizabethan form of the genitive (Abbott, *Shakespearean Grammar*
    228)

HIPPOLITO

  Brother I do applaud thy constant vengeance,
  The quaintness of thy malice, above thought.

VINDICE

  So 'tis laid on: now come and welcome duke,
  I have her for thee. I protest it brother,   110
  Methinks she makes almost as fair a sign
  As some old gentlewoman in a periwig.
  Hide thy face now for shame, thou hadst need have a mask
      now.
  'Tis vain when beauty flows, but when it fleets
  This would become graves better than the streets.   115

HIPPOLITO

  You have my voice in that. Hark, the duke's come.
                                    [*Noises within*]

VINDICE

  Peace – let's observe what company he brings
  And how he does absent 'em, for you know
  He'll wish all private. Brother fall you back a little
  With the bony lady.

HIPPOLITO   That I will.   [*He retires*]

VINDICE   So, so –   120
  Now nine years vengeance crowd into a minute.

            [*Enter the* DUKE *and gentlemen*]

DUKE

  You shall have leave to leave us, with this charge:
  Upon our lives, if we be missed by the duchess
  Or any of the nobles, to give out
  We're privately rid forth.

VINDICE   Oh happiness!   125

DUKE

  With some few honourable gentlemen, you may say:
  You may name those that are away from Court.

GENTLEMAN

  Your will and pleasure shall be done my lord.
                                  [*Exeunt gentlemen*]

VINDICE

  Privately rid forth?
  He strives to make sure work on't. [*Advances*] Your good
      Grace.   130

108 *quaintness* witty ingenuity
118 *absent* send away

DUKE

   Piato! well done. Hast brought her? What lady is't?

VINDICE

   Faith my lord a country lady, a little bashful at first as most
   of them are, but after the first kiss my lord the worst is past
   with them: your Grace knows now what you have to do.
   She's somewhat a grave look with her, but –   135

DUKE

   I love that best, conduct her.

VINDICE

   [*Aside*] Have at all.

DUKE

   In gravest looks the greatest faults seem less:
   Give me that sin that's robed in holiness.

VINDICE

   [*Aside*] Back with the torch; brother raise the perfumes.   140

DUKE

   How sweet can a duke breathe? Age has no fault.
   Pleasure should meet in a perfumed mist.
   Lady, sweetly encountered: I came from Court,
   I must be bold with you – oh! What's this? Oh!

                      [*He kisses the skull*]

VINDICE

   Royal villain, white devil!

DUKE   Oh!

VINDICE   Brother,   145

   Place the torch here that his affrighted eyeballs
   May start into those hollows. Duke, dost know
   Yon dreadful vizard? View it well; 'tis the skull
   Of Gloriana, whom thou poisonedst last.

DUKE

   Oh 't'as poisoned me!   150

VINDICE

   Didst not know that till now?

DUKE   What are you two?

VINDICE

   Villains all three! The very ragged bone
   Has been sufficiently revenged.

135 *She's* ed. (sha's Q) = She has
136 *grave look* Punning on the senses (i) serious expression, (ii) look of a corpse.
139 Possibly recalling Angelo's soliloquy in *Measure for Measure* II. ii. 164ff.
143–4 ed. (Lady … bould / with … this, oh / Q)
145–6 ed. (Royall … divill / Oh / Brother … eyeballs / Q)
145 *white* fair-seeming
147 *hollows* eye-sockets in the skull

DUKE

  Oh Hippolito – call treason!   [*Falls*]

HIPPOLITO

  Yes my good lord. Treason, treason, treason!   155

                              Stamping on him

DUKE

  Then I'm betrayed.

VINDICE

  Alas poor lecher: in the hands of knaves

  A slavish duke is baser than his slaves.

DUKE

  My teeth are eaten out.

VINDICE   Hadst any left?

HIPPOLITO

  I think but few.   160

VINDICE

  Then those that did eat are eaten.

DUKE   Oh my tongue!

VINDICE

  Your tongue? 'Twill teach you to kiss closer,

  Not like a slobbering Dutchman. You have eyes still:

  Look, monster, what a lady hast thou made me

  My once betrothed wife.

DUKE   Is it thou villain? Nay then –   165

VINDICE

  'Tis I, 'tis Vindice, 'tis I!

HIPPOLITO

  And let this comfort thee. Our lord and father

  Fell sick upon the infection of thy frowns

  And died in sadness. Be that thy hope of life.

DUKE   Oh!

VINDICE

  He had his tongue, yet grief made him die speechless.   170

  Puh, 'tis but early yet; now I'll begin

  To stick thy soul with ulcers; I will make

  Thy spirit grievous sore, it shall not rest

  But like some pestilent man, toss in thy breast.

161 Compare Hamlet's remark about the dead Polonius being 'Not where he eats, but where 'a is eaten' (*Hamlet* IV. iii. 19).

163 *slobbering* ed. (Flobbering Q). There is a word recorded in OED as 'flober' meaning 'to befoul', but the more likely sense, 'slobber', was at this time conveyed by 'slabber'. A MS form of *slabbering* could have been misread, or the printer may have picked the wrong fount, capital F and long s being very similar.

    Dutchman proverbial for drunkenness and general physical grossness

Mark me, duke,   175
Thou'rt a renowned, high, and mighty cuckold!
DUKE   Oh!
VINDICE
Thy bastard, thy bastard rides a-hunting in thy brow.
DUKE
Millions of deaths!
VINDICE   Nay to afflict thee more,
Here in this lodge they meet for damned clips:
Those eyes shall see the incest of their lips.   180
DUKE
Is there a hell besides this, villains?
VINDICE   Villain?
Nay heaven is just, scorns are the hires of scorns,
I ne'er knew yet adulterer without horns.
HIPPOLITO
Once ere they die 'tis quitted.   [*Noises within*]
VINDICE   Hark the music,
Their banquet is prepared, they're coming –   185
DUKE
Oh kill me not with that sight.
VINDICE
Thou shalt not lose that sight for all thy dukedom.
DUKE
Traitors, murderers!
VINDICE
What, is not thy tongue eaten out yet?
Then we'll invent a silence. Brother, stifle the torch.   190
DUKE
Treason! Murder!
VINDICE
Nay faith, we'll have you hushed now with thy dagger.
Nail down his tongue, and mine shall keep possession
About his heart; if he but gasp he dies,
We dread not death to quittance injuries. Brother,   195

175–6 ed. (*one line in* Q)
177 *rides* with a sexual meaning, as in I. ii. 136
177 *brow* Where the cuckold's horns sprout. Associated with reputation and honour
     at I. ii. 4 (and n.). See also IV. i. 22 below.
     clips embraces
192–4 Vindice's directions make precise and clear that the brothers station
     themselves on either side of the Duke, their daggers pointing at his treacherous
     tongue and false heart. The stage image has ironic and emblematic aptness. See
     also below IV. iv. 0sd and n.

If he but wink, not brooking the foul object
Let our two other hands tear up his lids
And make his eyes, like comets, shine through blood.
When the bad bleeds, then is the tragedy good.

HIPPOLITO

Whist brother, music's at our ear: they come.   200

Enter [SPURIO] *the bastard meeting the* DUCHESS

SPURIO

Had not that kiss a taste of sin 'twere sweet.

DUCHESS

Why there's no pleasure sweet but it is sinful.

SPURIO

True, such a bitter sweetness fate hath given;
Best side to us, is the worst side to heaven.

DUCHESS

Push, come, 'tis the old duke thy doubtful father –   205
The thought of him rubs heaven in thy way;
But I protest by yonder waxen fire,
Forget him or I'll poison him.

SPURIO

Madam you urge a thought which ne'er had life,
So deadly do I loathe him for my birth   210
That, if he took me hasped within his bed,
I would add murder to adultery
And with my sword give up his years to death.

DUCHESS

Why, now thou'rt sociable: let's in and feast.
Loudest music sound: pleasure is banquet's guest.   215

Exeunt [SPURIO *and* DUCHESS]

DUKE

I cannot brook –   [VINDICE *and* HIPPOLITO *kill the Duke*]

VINDICE   The brook is turned to blood.

196 *object* objection
197 *The Atheist's Tragedy* contains several references to the significance of portents
   in the heavens as signs of divine anger, especially IV. iii. 164–7:
            'How can earth endure
      The burden of this wickedness without
      An earthquake, or the angry face of Heav'n
      Be not enflam'd with lightning?'
206 *rubs* pushes (from the term in the game of bowls meaning to knock a bowl into
   an opponent's way)
207 *waxen fire* torch or candle
216 Punning on the verb meaning 'put up with' and noun 'stream'.
216 sd ed. (not in Q)

HIPPOLITO
    Thanks to loud music.
VINDICE   'Twas our friend indeed;
    'Tis state, in music for a duke to bleed.
    The dukedom wants a head, though yet unknown;
    As fast as they peep up let's cut 'em down.   *Exeunt*   220

[Act III, Scene vi]

Enter the duchess' two sons AMBITIOSO *and* SUPERVACUO

AMBITIOSO
    Was not his execution rarely plotted?
    We are the duke's sons now.
SUPERVACUO
    Ay, you may thank my policy for that.
AMBITIOSO
    Your policy for what?
SUPERVACUO
    Why was't not my invention brother   5
    To slip the judges, and, in lesser compass,
    Did not I draw the model of his death,
    Advising you to sudden officers
    And e'en extemporal execution?
AMBITIOSO
    Heart 'twas a thing I thought on too.   10
SUPERVACUO
    You thought on't too! 'Sfoot slander not your thoughts
    With glorious untruth: I know 'twas from you.
AMBITIOSO
    Sir I say 'twas in my head.
[SUPERVACUO]   Ay, like your brains then:
    Ne'er to come out as long as you lived.

219 though his death is not yet public knowledge
  1 The ironic design of the plot is emphasised here. Ambitioso's remark is about
     Lussurioso but, though he does not know it, it applies also to the killing of the
     Duke which the audience have just watched Vindice accomplish.
  6 *slip* evade
     in lesser compass of smaller importance or scope (The next line exploits the
     other sense of *compass*, a geometrical instrument.)
  8–9 recommending to you officers to carry out sudden – even summary – execu-
       tion
  12 *from you* not in your mind
  13 SUPERVACUO ed. (*Spu.* Q)

AMBITIOSO
    You'd have the honour on't forsooth that your wit   15
    Led him to the scaffold.
SUPERVACUO   Since it is my due
    I'll publish't – but I'll ha't, in spite of you.
AMBITIOSO
    Methinks y'are much too bold, you should a little
    Remember us brother, next to be honest duke.
SUPERVACUO
    [*Aside*] Ay, it shall be as easy for you to be duke   20
    As to be honest, and that's never i' faith.
AMBITIOSO
    Well, cold he is by this time, and because
    We're both ambitious be it our amity,
    And let the glory be shared equally.
SUPERVACUO
    I am content to that.   25
AMBITIOSO
    This night our younger brother shall out of prison:
    I have a trick.
SUPERVACUO   A trick? Prithee what is't?
AMBITIOSO
    We'll get him out by a wile.
SUPERVACUO   Prithee what wile?
AMBITIOSO
    No sir you shall not know it till it be done,
    For then you'd swear 'twere yours.   30

    [*Enter an officer with a bleeding head in his hand*]

SUPERVACUO
    How now, what's he?
AMBITIOSO   One of the officers.
SUPERVACUO
    Desired news.
AMBITIOSO   How now my friend?
OFFICER
    My lords, under your pardon, I am allotted
    To that desertless office to present you
    With the yet bleeding head –
SUPERVACUO [*Aside*]   Ha! Ha! Excellent!   35

---

19 i.e., that I am next in line for the honour of becoming Duke
21 *honest* Punning on the senses 'honourable' and 'virtuous'.
22 *he* i.e., Lussurioso

AMBITIOSO [*Aside*]
    All's sure our own – brother canst weep thinkst thou?
    'Twould grace our flattery much; think of some dame,
    'Twill teach thee to dissemble.
SUPERVACUO   I have thought –
    Now for yourself.
AMBITIOSO   Our sorrows are so fluent
    Our eyes o'erflow our tongues; words spoke in tears   40
    Are like the murmurs of the waters, the sound
    Is loudly heard but cannot be distinguished.
SUPERVACUO
    How died he pray?
OFFICER   Oh full of rage and spleen.
SUPERVACUO
    He died most valiantly then: we're glad
    To hear it.
OFFICER   We could not woo him once to pray.   45
AMBITIOSO
    He showed himself a gentleman in that,
    Give him his due.
OFFICER   But in the stead of prayer
    He drew forth oaths.
SUPERVACUO   Then did he pray dear heart,
    Although you understood him not.
OFFICER   My lords,
    E'en at his last – with pardon be it spoke –   50
    He cursed you both.
SUPERVACUO   He cursed us? 'Las, good soul.
AMBITIOSO
    It was not in our powers, but the duke's pleasure.
    [*Aside*] Finely dissembled o' both sides! Sweet fate,
    Oh happy opportunity!

Enter LUSSURIOSO

LUSSURIOSO   Now my lords –
AMBITIOSO & SUPERVACUO   Oh!
LUSSURIOSO
    Why do you shun me brothers? You may come nearer now,   55
    The savour of the prison has forsook me,
    I thank such kind lords as yourselves I'm free.

45 *woo* ed. (woe Q)
44–5 ed. (He ... it / We ... pray / Q)
46–7 ed. (He ... due / But ... oaths / Q)
55 ed. (Why ... Brothers / You ... now / Q)

AMBITIOSO
  Alive!
SUPERVACUO   In health!
AMBITIOSO   Released!
  We were both e'en amazed with joy to see it.
LUSSURIOSO
  I am much to thank you.   60
SUPERVACUO
  Faith we spared no tongue unto my lord the duke.
AMBITIOSO
  I know your delivery, brother,
  Had not been half so sudden but for us.
SUPERVACUO
  Oh how we pleaded.
LUSSURIOSO   Most deserving brothers;
  In my best studies I will think of it.   *Exit*   65
AMBITIOSO
  Oh death and vengeance!
SUPERVACUO   Hell and torments!
AMBITIOSO
  Slave! Cam'st thou to delude us?
OFFICER   Delude you my lords?
SUPERVACUO
  Ay villain: where's this head now?
OFFICER   Why here my lord;
  Just after his delivery you both came
  With warrant from the duke to behead your brother.   70
AMBITIOSO
  Ay, our brother, the duke's son.
OFFICER   The duke's son
  My lord, had his release before you came.
AMBITIOSO
  Whose head's that, then?
OFFICER   His, whom you left command for –
  Your own brother's.
AMBITIOSO   Our brother's? Oh furies!
SUPERVACUO
  Plagues!
AMBITIOSO Confusions!
SUPERVACUO   Darkness!
AMBITIOSO   Devils!   75
SUPERVACUO
  Fell it out so accursedly?
AMBITIOSO   So damnedly?

SUPERVACUO
  Villain I'll brain thee with it!
OFFICER   Oh my good lord!
SUPERVACUO
  The devil overtake thee!
AMBITIOSO   Oh fatal –
SUPERVACUO
  Oh prodigious to our bloods!
AMBITIOSO   Did we dissemble?
SUPERVACUO
  Did we make our tears women for thee?   80
AMBITIOSO
  Laugh and rejoice for thee?
SUPERVACUO
  Bring warrant for thy death?
AMBITIOSO
  Mock off thy head?
SUPERVACUO
  You had a trick, you had a wile forsooth.
AMBITIOSO
  A murrain meet 'em! There's none of these wiles that ever   85
  come to good. I see now there is nothing sure in mortality
  but mortality.
  Well, no more words – shalt be revenged i' faith.
  Come throw off clouds now brother; think of vengeance
  And deeper settled hate. Sirrah sit fast: 90
  We'll pull down all, but thou shalt down at last.   *Exeunt*

Act IV, Scene i

Enter LUSSURIOSO *with* HIPPOLITO

LUSSURIOSO
  Hippolito.
HIPPOLITO
  My lord:
  Has your good lordship aught to command me in?
LUSSURIOSO
  I prithee leave us.
HIPPOLITO   How's this! Come, and leave us?

  85 *murrain* plague
  90 *Sirrah* i.e., Lussurioso
   3 *Aught* ed. (ought Q)

LUSSURIOSO
  Hippolito.   5
HIPPOLITO
  Your honour, I stand ready for any dutious employment.
LUSSURIOSO
  Heart, what mak'st thou here?
HIPPOLITO [*Aside*]   A pretty lordly humour:
  He bids me to be present; to depart;
  Something has stung his honour.
LUSSURIOSO   Be nearer, draw nearer;
  You're not so good methinks, I'm angry with you.   10
HIPPOLITO
  With me my lord? I'm angry with myself for't.
LUSSURIOSO
  You did prefer a goodly fellow to me:
  'Twas wittily elected, 'twas – I thought
  He'd been a villain, and he proves a knave!
  To me a knave!
HIPPOLITO   I chose him for the best my lord: 15
  'Tis much my sorrow if neglect in him
  Breed discontent in you.
LUSSURIOSO   Neglect? 'Twas will: judge of it:
  Firmly to tell of an incredible act
  Not to be thought, less to be spoken of,
  'Twixt my stepmother and the bastard – oh,   20
  Incestuous sweets between 'em!
HIPPOLITO   Fie my lord.
LUSSURIOSO
  I, in kind loyalty to my father's forehead,
  Made this a desperate arm, and in that fury
  Committed treason on the lawful bed
  And with my sword e'en razed my father's bosom,   25
  For which I was within a stroke of death.
HIPPOLITO
  Alack, I'm sorry. [*Aside*] 'Sfoot, just upon the stroke
  Jars in my brother: 'twill be villainous music!

Enter VINDICE [*disguised*]

  8–9 ed. (He . . . honour / Be . . . neerer / Q)
  14 *He'd* ed. (Had Q)
  16–17 ed. (Tis . . . you / Neglect . . . it / Q)
  22 *forehead* See III. v. 177 and n.
  25 *razed* grazed (as with razor)
  28 *Jars* interrupts discordantly

VINDICE
  My honoured lord.
LUSSURIOSO
  Away prithee, forsake us: hereafter we'll not know thee.   30
VINDICE
  Not know me my lord? Your lordship cannot choose.
LUSSURIOSO
  Begone I say, thou art a false knave.
VINDICE
  Why, the easier to be known my lord.
LUSSURIOSO
  Push, I shall prove too bitter with a word,
  Make thee a perpetual prisoner   35
  And lay this iron-age upon thee.
VINDICE [*Aside*]   Mum,
  For there's a doom would make a woman dumb.
  Missing the bastard next him, the wind's come about;
  Now 'tis my brother's turn to stay, mine to go out.
                                          Exit VINDICE
LUSSURIOSO
  Has greatly moved me.
HIPPOLITO   Much to blame i' faith.   40
LUSSURIOSO
  But I'll recover, to his ruin. 'Twas told me lately,
  I know not whether falsely, that you'd a brother.
HIPPOLITO
  Who I? Yes my good lord, I have a brother.
LUSSURIOSO
  How chance the Court ne'er saw him? Of what nature?
  How does he apply his hours?
HIPPOLITO   Faith to curse Fates   45
  Who, as he thinks, ordained him to be poor;
  Keeps at home full of want and discontent.
LUSSURIOSO
  There's hope in him, for discontent and want
  Is the best clay to mould a villain of.
  Hippolito, wish him repair to us.   50
  If there be aught in him to please our blood

36 *iron-age* (i) imprisonment in iron fetters, (ii) fettering lasting an Age of Iron,
  the last and worst of the mythical four Ages (Gold, Silver and Brass being the
  first three)
36-7 ed. (And ... thee / Mum ... dum / Q)
38 *come* ed. (comes Q)
50 *repair* make his way
51 *blood* desire, temper (with allusion to Lussurioso's boasted proud breeding)

For thy sake we'll advance him, and build fair
His meanest fortunes; for it is in us
To rear up towers from cottages.
HIPPOLITO
It is so my lord; he will attend your honour,   55
But he's a man in whom much melancholy dwells.
LUSSURIOSO
Why the better: bring him to Court.
HIPPOLITO
With willingness and speed. [*Aside*] Whom he cast off
E'en now, must now succeed. Brother disguise must off;
In thine own shape now I'll prefer thee to him: 60
How strangely does himself work to undo him.   *Exit*
LUSSURIOSO
This fellow will come fitly; he shall kill
That other slave that did abuse my spleen
And made it swell to treason. I have put
Much of my heart into him; he must die.   65
He that knows great men's secrets, and proves slight,
That man ne'er lives to see his beard turn white.
Ay, he shall speed him: I'll employ thee brother,
Slaves are but nails to drive out one another.
He being of black condition, suitable   70
To want and ill content, hope of preferment
Will grind him to an edge.

The nobles enter

1 NOBLE
Good days unto your honour.
LUSSURIOSO   My kind lords,
I do return the like.
2 NOBLE   Saw you my lord the duke?
LUSSURIOSO
My lord and father: is he from Court?   75

---

59 *succeed* be the successor
58–9 ed. (With . . . speed / Whom . . . succeed / Brother . . . off / Q)
61 *himself . . . him* he strives to achieve his own undoing
66 *slight* not trustworthy
68 *speed* i.e., kill
69 Alluding to the proverb (Tilley N 17).
70 *black* melancholic
72 sd printed as the continuation of line 70 in Q
73–5 ed. (Good . . . honour / My . . . like / Sawe . . . Duke / Q)

1 NOBLE

　He's sure from Court, but where, which way his pleasure
　took, we know not nor can we hear on't.

　　　　　　　[*Enter other nobles*]

LUSSURIOSO

　Here come those should tell – saw you my lord and father?

3 NOBLE

　Not since two hours before noon my lord, and then he
　privately rid forth.　　　　　　　　　　　　　　　　　　80

LUSSURIOSO

　Oh he's rode forth.

1 NOBLE　　　　　　　　'Twas wondrous privately.

2 NOBLE

　There's none i' the Court had any knowledge on't.

LUSSURIOSO

　His Grace is old, and sudden, 'tis no treason
　To say the duke my father has a humour,
　Or such a toy, about him; what in us　　　　　　　　　85
　Would appear light, in him seems virtuous.

3 NOBLE

　'Tis oracle my lord.　　　　　　　　　　　　*Exeunt*

[Act IV, Scene ii]

Enter VINDICE *and* HIPPOLITO (VINDICE *out of his disguise*)

HIPPOLITO

　So, so, all's as it should be, y'are yourself.

VINDICE

　How that great villain puts me to my shifts!

HIPPOLITO

　He that did lately in disguise reject thee
　Shall, now thou art thyself, as much respect thee.

VINDICE

　'Twill be the quainter fallacy; but brother,　　　　　　5
　'Sfoot, what use will he put me to now, think'st thou?

HIPPOLITO

　Nay you must pardon me in that, I know not;

76–7 ed. (Hees ... Court / But ... know not / Nor ... ont / Q)
79–80 ed. (Not ... Lord / And ... forth / Q)
81 *rode* (rod Q)
　2 *shifts* (i) tricks, (ii) disguises

H'as some employment for you, but what 'tis
He and his secretary the devil knows best.
VINDICE
Well I must suit my tongue to his desires   10
What colour soe'er they be, hoping at last
To pile up all my wishes on his breast.
HIPPOLITO
Faith brother he himself shows the way.
VINDICE
Now the duke is dead the realm is clad in clay;
His death being not yet known, under his name   15
The people still are governed; well, thou his son
Art not long-lived, thou shalt not 'joy his death:
To kill thee then I should most honour thee,
For 'twould stand firm in every man's belief
Thou'st a kind child, and only diedst with grief.   20
HIPPOLITO
You fetch about well; but let's talk in present.
How will you appear in fashion different,
As well as in apparel, to make all things possible?
If you be but once tripped we fall for ever.
It is not the least policy to be doubtful;   25
You must change tongue – familiar was your first.
VINDICE
Why I'll bear me in some strain of melancholy
And string myself with heavy sounding wire
Like such an instrument that speaks
Merry things sadly.
HIPPOLITO   Then 'tis as I meant,   30
I gave you out at first in discontent.
VINDICE
I'll turn myself, and then –

[*Enter* LUSSURIOSO]

HIPPOLITO   'Sfoot here he comes –
Hast thought upon't?
VINDICE   Salute him, fear not me.
LUSSURIOSO
Hippolito.
HIPPOLITO
Your lordship.   35

21 *in present* i.e., in terms of the present
25 it is not the worst policy to anticipate trouble
29–33 ed. (Like . . . sadly / Then . . . meant / I . . . discontent / Ile . . . then / Sfoote . . .
    vppont / Salute . . . me / Q)

LUSSURIOSO
  What's he yonder?
HIPPOLITO
  'Tis Vindice my discontented brother,
  Whom, 'cording to your will I've brought to Court.
LUSSURIOSO
  Is that thy brother? Beshrew me a good presence;
  I wonder h'as been from the Court so long.   40
  Come nearer.
HIPPOLITO
  Brother: lord Lussurioso the duke's son.
LUSSURIOSO
  Be more near to us: welcome, nearer yet.
VINDICE
  How don you? God you god den.
              [VINDICE] *snatches off his hat and [bows] to him*
LUSSURIOSO   We thank thee.
  How strangely such a coarse, homely salute   45
  Shows in the palace, where we greet in fire –
  Nimble and desperate tongues! Should we name
  God in a salutation 'twould ne'er be 'stood on't – heaven!
  Tell me, what has made thee so melancholy.
VINDICE
  Why going to law.   50
LUSSURIOSO
  Why, will that make a man melancholy?
VINDICE
  Yes, to look long upon ink and black buckram. I went me to
  law in *anno quadragesimo secundo*, and I waded out of it in
  anno sextagesimo tertio.
LUSSURIOSO
  What, three and twenty years in law?   55
VINDICE
  I have known those that have been five and fifty, and all
  about pullin and pigs.
LUSSURIOSO
  May it be possible such men should breathe to vex the
  terms so much?

48 *'twould ... on't* it would never be understood as such
53 *anno ... secundo* forty-second
54 *anno ... tertio* sixty-third
57 *pullin* poultry
58 *terms* the four terms in the year when the law-courts sit
58–9 ed. (May ... breath / To ... much / Q)

VINDICE

'Tis food to some my lord. There are old men at the present   60
that are so poisoned with the affectation of law words,
having had many suits canvassed, that their common talk is
nothing but Barbary Latin; they cannot so much as pray,
but in law, that their sins may be removed with a writ of
Error, and their souls fetched up to heaven with a sasarara.   65

[LUSSURIOSO]

It seems most strange to me;
Yet all the world meets round in the same bent:
Where the heart's set, there goes the tongue's consent.
How dost apply thy studies fellow?

VINDICE

Study? Why, to think how a great rich man lies a-dying, and   70
a poor cobbler tolls the bell for him; how he cannot depart
the world, and see the great chest stand before him; when
he lies speechless, how he will point you readily to all the
boxes, and when he is past all memory, as the gossips guess,
then thinks he of forfeitures and obligations. Nay, when to   75
all men's hearings he whirls and rattles in the throat, he's
busy threatening his poor tenants; and this would last me
now some seven years thinking, or thereabouts! But I have
a conceit a-coming in picture upon this, I draw it myself,
which i' faith la I'll present to your honour; you shall not   80
choose but like it for your lordship shall give me nothing
for it.

LUSSURIOSO

Nay you mistake me then,
For I am published bountiful enough;
Let's taste of your conceit.   85

VINDICE

In picture my lord?

LUSSURIOSO

Ay, in picture.

VINDICE

Marry this it is: 'A usuring father to be boiling in hell, and
his son and heir with a whore dancing over him'.

HIPPOLITO

[*Aside*] H'as pared him to the quick.   90

60 on a fresh line, Q corrected (continuing line 57, Q uncorrected)
63 *Barbary* barbarous
65 *sasarara* i.e., certiorari, a writ issued by a superior court when a plaintiff claims
  injustice from a lower court
88 *usuring ... hell* the punishment traditionally believed to apply to usurers. See
  plate 4 in the Introduction above, p. xv.

LUSSURIOSO
  The conceit's pretty i' faith – but take't upon my life 'twill
  ne'er be liked.
VINDICE
  No? Why I'm sure the whore will be liked well enough!
HIPPOLITO
  [*Aside*] Ay, if she were out o' the picture he'd like her then
  himself.   95
VINDICE
  And as for the son and heir, he shall be an eyesore to no
  young revellers, for he shall be drawn in cloth of gold
  breeches.
LUSSURIOSO
  And thou hast put my meaning in the pockets
  And canst not draw that out. My thought was this: 100
  To see the picture of a usuring father
  Boiling in hell – our rich men would ne'er like it.
VINDICE
  Oh true, I cry you heartily mercy; I know the reason: for
  some of 'em had rather be damned indeed than damned in
  colours.   105
LUSSURIOSO
  [*Aside*] A parlous melancholy! H'as wit enough
  To murder any man, and I'll give him means. –
  I think thou art ill-moneyed?
VINDICE   Money! Ho, ho.
  'T'as been my want so long 'tis now my scoff;
  I've e'en forgot what colour silver's of!   110
LUSSURIOSO
  [*Aside*] It hits as I could wish.
VINDICE   I get good clothes
  Of those that dread my humour, and for table room
  I feed on those that cannot be rid of me.
LUSSURIOSO
  [*Giving* VINDICE *money*] Somewhat to set thee up withal.
VINDICE
  Oh mine eyes!
LUSSURIOSO   How now man?
VINDICE   Almost struck blind!   115
  This bright unusual shine to me seems proud:
  I dare not look till the sun be in a cloud.

91–92 ed. (The ... ifaith / But ... likt / Q)
105 *colours* (i) in a painting, (ii) in mere seeming, appearance

LUSSURIOSO
  [*Aside*] I think I shall affect his melancholy; –
  How are they now?
VINDICE   The better for your asking.
LUSSURIOSO
  You shall be better yet if you but fasten   120
  Truly on my intent. Now y'are both present
  I will unbrace such a close private villain
  Unto your vengeful swords, the like ne'er heard of,
  Who hath disgraced you much and injured us.
HIPPOLITO
  Disgraced us my lord?
LUSSURIOSO   Ay, Hippolito.   125
  I kept it here till now that both your angers
  Might meet him at once.
VINDICE   I'm covetous
  To know the villain.
LUSSURIOSO   You know him – that slave pandar
  Piato, whom we threatened last
  With irons in perpetual prisonment.   130
VINDICE
  [*Aside*] All this is I!
HIPPOLITO   Is't he my lord?
LUSSURIOSO   I'll tell you –
  You first preferred him to me.
VINDICE [*Aside*]   Did you brother?
HIPPOLITO
  I did indeed.
LUSSURIOSO   And the ungrateful villain
  To quit that kindness strongly wrought with me,
  Being as you see a likely man for pleasure,   135
  With jewels to corrupt your virgin sister.
HIPPOLITO
  Oh villain!
VINDICE   He shall surely die that did it.
LUSSURIOSO
  I, far from thinking any virgin harm,
  Especially knowing her to be as chaste
  As that part which scarce suffers to be touched,   140
  The eye, would not endure him, –
VINDICE   Would you not my lord?
  'Twas wondrous honourably done.

118. *affect* like

LUSSURIOSO
  But with some fine frowns kept him out.
VINDICE   Out slave!
LUSSURIOSO
  What did me he but in revenge of that
  Went of his own free will to make infirm   145
  Your sister's honour, whom I honour with my soul
  For chaste respect; and, not prevailing there
  – As 'twas but desperate folly to attempt it –
  In mere spleen, by the way, waylays your mother,
  Whose honour being a coward as it seems,   150
  Yielded by little force.
VINDICE   Coward indeed.
LUSSURIOSO
  He, proud of this advantage, as he thought,
  Brought me these news for happy; but I
  – Heaven forgive me for't –
VINDICE   What did your honour?
LUSSURIOSO
  In rage pushed him from me,   155
  Trampled beneath his throat, spurned him and bruised;
  Indeed I was too cruel, to say truth.
HIPPOLITO
  Most nobly managed.
VINDICE
  [*Aside*] Has not heaven an ear? Is all the lightning wasted?
LUSSURIOSO
  If I now were so impatient in a modest cause,   160
  What should you be?
VINDICE   Full mad: he shall not live
  To see the moon change.
LUSSURIOSO   He's about the palace.
  Hippolito, entice him this way, that thy brother
  May take full mark of him.

143 *fine* ed. (five Q)
152 *this* ed. (their Q)
153 ed. (Brought . . . for't / Q)
159 *Is . . . wasted* Compare the discussion about thunder's intervention in human
    affairs in Tourneur, *The Atheist's Tragedy* II. iv. 140–55, or in Chettle, *Tragedy
    of Hoffman* I. i, where Hoffman has thunder's support:
      'Ill acts move some, but myne's a cause that's right
        Thunder and Lightning
      See the powers of heaven in apparitions/ . . . incensed'

HIPPOLITO
    Heart! That shall not need my lord,   165
    I can direct him so far.
LUSSURIOSO   Yet for my hate's sake
    Go, wind him this way; I'll see him bleed myself.
HIPPOLITO
    [*Aside*] What now brother?
VINDICE
    [*Aside*] Nay e'en what you will; y'are put to't, brother?
HIPPOLITO
    [*Aside*] An impossible task I'll swear,   170
    To bring him hither that's already here.   *Exit* HIPPOLITO
LUSSURIOSO
    Thy name? I have forgot it.
VINDICE   Vindice my lord.
LUSSURIOSO
    'Tis a good name, that.
VINDICE   Ay, a revenger.
LUSSURIOSO
    It does betoken courage, thou shouldst be valiant
    And kill thine enemies.
VINDICE   That's my hope my lord.   175
LUSSURIOSO
    This slave is one.
VINDICE   I'll doom him.
LUSSURIOSO   Then I'll praise thee.
    Do thou observe me best and I'll best raise thee.

                    Enter HIPPOLITO

VINDICE
    Indeed I thank you.
LUSSURIOSO   Now Hippolito,
    Where's the slave pandar?
HIPPOLITO   Your good lordship would have
    A loathsome sight of him, much offensive?   180
    He's not in case now to be seen my lord,
    The worst of all the deadly sins is in him:
    That beggarly damnation, drunkenness.

---

167 *wind* entice, draw
177 *observe* serve, follow
178–80 ed.   (Indeed . . . you / Now . . . Pandar / Your . . . Lordship / Would . . . of-
    fensive / Q)
181 *in case* in a condition (and punning on the sense *case* = mask, disguise, costume,
    as in *Measure for Measure* II. iv. 12–13)

LUSSURIOSO
  Then he's a double slave.
VINDICE [*Aside*]   'Twas well conveyed,
  Upon a sudden wit.
LUSSURIOSO   What, are you both   185
  Firmly resolved? I'll see him dead myself!
VINDICE
  Or else let not us live.
LUSSURIOSO   You may direct
  Your brother to take note of him.
HIPPOLITO   I shall.
LUSSURIOSO
  Rise but in this and you shall never fall.
VINDICE
  Your honour's vassals.
LUSSURIOSO [*Aside*]   This was wisely carried;   190
  Deep policy in us makes fools of such:
  Then must a slave die, when he knows too much.
                                   Exit LUSSURIOSO
VINDICE
  Oh thou almighty patience 'tis my wonder,
  That such a fellow, impudent and wicked,
  Should not be cloven as he stood   195
  Or with a secret wind burst open!
  Is there no thunder left, or is't kept up
  In stock for heavier vengeance? [*Thunder*] There it goes!
HIPPOLITO
  Brother we lose ourselves.
VINDICE   But I have found it,
  'Twill hold, 'tis sure, thanks, thanks to any spirit   200
  That mingled it 'mongst my inventions.
HIPPOLITO
  What is't?
VINDICE   'Tis sound and good, thou shalt partake it,
  I'm hired to kill myself.
HIPPOLITO   True.
VINDICE   Prithee mark it;
  And the old duke being dead but not conveyed
  – For he's already missed too – and you know   205
  Murder will peep out of the closest husk –

184–7 ed. (Then ... double-slave / Twas ... wit / What ... both / Firmely ... selfe /
    Or ... live / You ... him / Q)
199 *found it* thought up a solution

HIPPOLITO
  Most true!
VINDICE   What say you then to this device:
  If we dressed up the body of the duke –
HIPPOLITO
  In that disguise of yours!
VINDICE   Y'are quick, y'ave reached it.
HIPPOLITO
  I like it wondrously.   210
VINDICE
  And being in drink, as you have published him,
  To lean him on his elbow as if sleep had caught him
  – Which claims most interest in such sluggy men.
HIPPOLITO
  Good yet; but here's a doubt.
  We thought by th' duke's son to kill that pandar,   215
  Shall, when he is known, be thought to kill the duke.
VINDICE
  Neither, oh thanks! It is substantial; for that disguise being
  on him, which I wore, it will be thought I, which he calls the
  pandar, did kill the duke and fled away in his apparel,
  leaving him so disguised to avoid swift pursuit.   220
HIPPOLITO
  Firmer and firmer.
VINDICE   Nay doubt not, 'tis in grain,
  I warrant it hold colour.
HIPPOLITO   Let's about it.
VINDICE
  But by the way too, now I think on't, brother,
  Let's conjure that base devil out of our mother.   *Exeunt*

---

212 The idea of arranging the corpse in a life-like way ingeniously varies the device
    of the bony lady in III. v, which in turn reversed the image of the dead wife of
    Antonio in I. iv.
215 *We* ed. (Me Q)
221-2 i.e., it is sound and will hold firmly (For the metaphor of colour being fast-
    dyed rather than soluble, on the mere surface, see *Twelfth Night* I. v. 237–8.)
    Another instance of the images of painting, especially face-painting, which
    abound in the play. Male as well as female courtiers used face-paint in the
    Jacobean period.
221-2 ed. (Nay...collour / Lets about it / Q)

[Act IV, Scene iii]

Enter the DUCHESS *arm in arm with the bastard* [SPURIO]: *he seemeth lasciviously to her; after them enter* SUPERVACUO *running with a rapier: his brother* [AMBITIOSO] *stops him*

SPURIO
  Madam unlock yourself; should it be seen
  Your arm would be suspected.
DUCHESS
  Who is't that dares suspect or this, or these?
  May not we deal our favours where we please?
SPURIO
  I'm confident you may.

Exeunt [SPURIO and DUCHESS]

AMBITIOSO   'Sfoot brother hold!   5
SUPERVACUO
  Wouldst let the bastard shame us?
AMBITIOSO   Hold, hold brother!
  There's fitter time than now.
SUPERVACUO   Now, when I see it!
AMBITIOSO
  'Tis too much seen already.
SUPERVACUO   Seen and known:
  The nobler she is, the baser is she grown.
AMBITIOSO
  If she were bent lasciviously – the fault   10
  Of mighty women that sleep soft – Oh death
  Must she needs choose such an unequal sinner
  To make all worse?
SUPERVACUO
  A bastard! The duke's bastard! Shame heaped on shame!
AMBITIOSO
  Oh our disgrace!
  Most women have small waist the world throughout,   15
  But their desires are thousand miles about.
SUPERVACUO
  Come, stay not here: let's after and prevent:
  Or else they'll sin faster than we'll repent.   *Exeunt*

  3 *this, or these* Presumably she gives him further caresses or kisses.
  6 *Wouldst* (Woult Q)
  6–7 ed. (Woult . . . us / Hold . . . now / Q)
  10 *bent lasciviously* determined to be lascivious
  15 *waist* ed. (waste Q)
  17–18 Uncorrected copies reverse the order of these lines; corrected copies
      misplace *Exeunt* after line 18.

[Act IV, Scene iv]

Enter VINDICE *and* HIPPOLITO *bringing out their mother*
[GRATIANA,] *one by one shoulder, and the other by the other,*
with daggers in their hands

VINDICE
  O thou for whom no name is bad enough!
GRATIANA
  What means my sons? What, will you murder me?
VINDICE
  Wicked, unnatural parent!
HIPPOLITO   Fiend of women!
GRATIANA
  Oh! Are sons turned monsters? Help!
VINDICE   In vain.
GRATIANA
  Are you so barbarous, to set iron nipples   5
  Upon the breast that gave you suck?
VINDICE   That breast
  Is turned to quarled poison.
GRATIANA
  Cut not your days for't: am not I your mother?
VINDICE
  Thou dost usurp that title now by fraud,
  For in that shell of mother breeds a bawd.   10
GRATIANA
  A bawd! Oh name far loathsomer than hell!
HIPPOLITO
  It should be so, knew'st thou thy office well.
GRATIANA
  I hate it.

---

  0 sd The brothers, either side of their mother, daggers drawn, present a visual
      parallel to their seizing of the Duke: see III. v. 192–4 and n. Their interrogation
      of their mother recalls *Hamlet* III. iv.
  3 *parent* ed. (parents Q)
  7 *quarled* curdled
  8 *cut . . . days* i.e., do not shorten your life (See II. ii. 95 where Exodus 20:12 is
      invoked.)
  12 *knewst* Q corrected (knowst Q uncorrected)
      office maternal duty

VINDICE

    Ah is't possible, thou only – you powers on high,
    That women should dissemble when they die?   15

GRATIANA

    Dissemble?

VINDICE   Did not the duke's son direct

    A fellow of the world's condition hither
    That did corrupt all that was good in thee,
    Made thee uncivilly forget thyself
    And work our sister to his lust?

GRATIANA   Who, I?   20

    That had been monstrous! I defy that man
    For any such intent. None lives so pure
    But shall be soiled with slander –
    Good son believe it not.

VINDICE   Oh I'm in doubt

    Whether I'm myself or no!   25
    Stay – let me look again upon this face:
    Who shall be saved when mothers have no grace?

HIPPOLITO

    'Twould make one half despair.

VINDICE   I was the man:

    Defy me now! Let's see: do't modestly.

GRATIANA

    Oh hell unto my soul.   30

VINDICE

    In that disguise, I, sent from the duke's son,
    Tried you, and found you base metal
    As any villain might have done.

GRATIANA   Oh no:

    No tongue but yours could have bewitched me so.

VINDICE

    Oh nimble in damnation, quick in tune: 35

---

14 *thou only* ed. (*printed in italic in* Q). Swinburne, cited by Nicoll, suggested that
the line originally read 'Ah ist possible Thou onely God on hie'. Either in the
playhouse or the printinghouse this was emended, 'Thou onely God' being
crossed out and 'you powers' written in above. The compositor misunderstood
the MS and printed 'thou onely'. Nicoll emends with a compromise, 'Ah ist
possible, you [heavenly] powers on hie', to restore metre, accepting Swinburne's
conjecture. A number of playscripts at this time witness deference to the new
(1606) Act to Restrain the Abuses of Players, which forbade direct references to
the Deity.

23–4 ed. (But . . . not / Oh . . . doubt / Q)

32 Alluding to the proving or testing of precious metals for purity. Gold was
assayed or tried with a touchstone and stamped if found true.

33–4 ed. (As . . . done / O no . . . so / Q)

There is no devil could strike fire so soon!
I am confuted in a word.

GRATIANA   Oh sons
Forgive me, to myself I'll prove more true;
You that should honour me – I kneel to you.

[She kneels and weeps]

VINDICE

A mother to give aim to her own daughter!   40

HIPPOLITO

True brother: how far beyond nature 'tis,
Though many mothers do't!

VINDICE

Nay and you draw tears once, go you to bed;
Wet will make iron blush and change to red:
Brother it rains, 'twill spoil your dagger, house it.   45

HIPPOLITO

'Tis done.

VINDICE

I' faith 'tis a sweet shower, it does much good;
The fruitful grounds and meadows of her soul
Has been long dry. Pour down, thou blessed dew.
Rise mother; troth this shower has made you higher.   50

GRATIANA

Oh you heavens,
Take this infectious spot out of my soul!
I'll rinse it in seven waters of mine eyes;
Make my tears salt enough to taste of grace;

37-8 ed. (I . . . word / Oh . . . true / Q)

39 In a society where parental authority was so strong, a parent's submission to a
child was a deep and disturbing breach of custom. See *King Lear* and Lear's
mock-kneeling to Regan and Goneril, his daughters, II. iv. 154–5, and his later
contrition with Cordelia, V. iii. 10–11.

40 *give aim* i.e., guide her daughter to seduce someone

41 *'tis* Q corrected (to't Q uncorrected)

44 *Wet . . . yron . . . red* Q corrected 2 (Wet . . . you . . . red Q corrected 1;
Wee . . . you . . . red Q uncorrected)
This line exists in three states, and it is difficult to be sure of their order. I
suppose Vindice to be talking to his dagger. Tempered steel is susceptible to
rusting (Othello says 'Keep up your bright swords, for the dew will rust them'
(I. ii. 59), but the added conceit is that the dagger-blade will reflect the mother's
shame, expressed in tears and blushes.

45 *it rains* Referring to Gratiana's tears.

47-8 *shower . . . meadows* Recalling, but with different effect, the images of
I. iii. 50–4.

52 *infectious* infected

To weep is to our sex naturally given,   55
But to weep truly – that's a gift from heaven!
VINDICE
Nay I'll kiss you now; kiss her, brother,
Let's marry her to our souls, wherein's no lust,
And honourably love her.
HIPPOLITO   Let it be.
VINDICE
For honest women are so seld and rare,   60
'Tis good to cherish those poor few that are.
Oh you of easy wax, do but imagine
Now the disease has left you, how leprously
That office would have clinged unto your forehead.
All mothers that had any graceful hue   65
Would have worn masks to hide their face at you.
It would have grown to this, at your foul name
Green-coloured maids would have turned red with shame.
HIPPOLITO
And then, our sister full of hire and baseness –
VINDICE
There had been boiling lead again!   70
The duke's son's great concubine!
A drab of state, a cloth o' silver slut,
To have her train borne up and her soul
Trail i' the dirt: great!
HIPPOLITO   To be miserably great:
Rich, to be eternally wretched.   75
VINDICE
O common madness:
Ask but the thriving'st harlot in cold blood,
She'd give the world to make her honour good.
Perhaps you'll say, but only to the duke's son
In private – why, she first begins with one   80

60 *seld* ed. (sild Q)=rare
63-4 *leprously...forehead* See *Hamlet* III. iv. 42–4:
          'takes off the rose
     From the fair forehead of an innocent love
     And sets a blister there'.
68 *Green-coloured* very young, inexperienced
69 *hire* payment for services as a whore
71 *The duke's* Q corrected (dukes Q uncorrected)
73-5 ed. (To ... durt; great / To be ... wretched / Q; A cloth ... train / Borne ...
     dirt ... great / To be ... be / Eternally ... madness / *Foakes*)
74 *To be* Q corrected (Too Q uncorrected)

Who afterward to thousand proves a whore:
'Break ice in one place it will crack in more.'
GRATIANA
Most certainly applied!
HIPPOLITO
Oh brother you forgot our business.
VINDICE
And well remembered: joy's a subtle elf,   85
I think man's happiest when he forgets himself.
Farewell once dried, now holy-watered mead:
Our hearts wear feathers that before wore lead.
GRATIANA
I'll give you this: that one I never knew
Plead better for, and 'gainst the devil, than you.   90
VINDICE
You make me proud on't.
HIPPOLITO
Commend us in all virtue to our sister.
VINDICE
Ay for the love of heaven, to that true maid.
GRATIANA
With my best words.
VINDICE   Why that was motherly said.
                    Exeunt [VINDICE *and* HIPPOLITO]

GRATIANA
I wonder now what fury did transport me;   95
I feel good thoughts begin to settle in me.
Oh with what forehead can I look on her
Whose honour I've so impiously beset
– And here she comes.

                    [*Enter* CASTIZA]

CASTIZA
Now mother you have wrought with me so strongly   100
That what for my advancement, as to calm
The trouble of your tongue, I am content –
GRATIANA
Content to what?
CASTIZA   To do as you have wished me,
To prostitute my breast to the duke's son
And put myself to common usury.   105

---

82 This sententious remark is not cited as proverbial in Tilley but its meaning is
   clear: chastity is proverbially cold as ice.
97 *forehead* See lines 63–4 and n. above.

GRATIANA
  I hope you will not so.
CASTIZA   Hope you I will not?
  That's not the hope you look to be saved in.
GRATIANA
  Truth but it is.
CASTIZA   Do not deceive yourself:
  I am, as you, e'en out of marble wrought:
  What would you now, are ye not pleased yet with me?   110
  You shall not wish me to be more lascivious
  Than I intend to be.
GRATIANA   Strike not me cold.
CASTIZA
  How often have you charged me on your blessing
  To be a cursed woman! When you knew
  Your blessing had no force to make me lewd   115
  You laid your curse upon me. That did more
  – The mother's curse is heavy; where that fights,
  Sons set in storm and daughters lose their lights.
GRATIANA
  Good child, dear maid, if there be any spark
  Of heavenly intellectual fire within thee,   120
  Oh let my breath revive it to a flame:
  Put not all out with woman's wilful follies,
  I am recovered of that foul disease
  That haunts too many mothers: kind, forgive me,
  Make me not sick in health. If then   125
  My words prevailed when they were wickedness,
  How much more now when they are just and good!
CASTIZA
  I wonder what you mean: are not you she
  For whose infect persuasions I could scarce
  Kneel out my prayers, and had much ado   130
  In three hours' reading to untwist so much
  Of the black serpent as you wound about me?

---

109 *marble* i.e., impervious to shame (See I. iii. 8, 'dauntless marble'.)

118 i.e., sons and daughters end in damnation (punning on sons/*suns* and on *lights*:
    (i) spiritual guidance, (ii) heavenly bodies, sun, moon, stars)

120–21 ed. (Of... breath / Revive ... flame / Q)

124 *kind, forgive* ed. (kind forgive Q). The comma emphasises that *kind* is a term of
    address, 'kind one'. The mother commends her daughter as *loving*, as *close kin*,
    and as *natural* (not unnatural).

125 *sick in health* i.e., spiritually distressed though physically well

131 *reading* i.e., in devotional works and prayers

GRATIANA
   'Tis unfruitful, held tedious, to repeat what's past:
   I'm now your present mother.
CASTIZA   Push, now 'tis too late.
GRATIANA
   Bethink again, thou know'st not what thou say'st.   135
CASTIZA
   No – deny advancement, treasure, the duke's son?
GRATIANA
   Oh see, I spoke those words, and now they poison me:
   What will the deed do then?
   Advancement? True: as high as shame can pitch;
   For treasure? Who e'er knew a harlot rich   140
   Or could build by the purchase of her sin
   An hospital to keep their bastards in?
   The duke's son! Oh when women are young courtiers
   They are sure to be old beggars;
   To know the miseries most harlots taste   145
   Thou'd'st wish thyself unborn when thou art unchaste.
CASTIZA
   Oh mother let me twine about your neck
   And kiss you till my soul melt on your lips:
   I did but this to try you.
GRATIANA   Oh speak truth!
CASTIZA
   Indeed I did not; for no tongue has force   150
   To alter me from honest.
   If maidens would, men's words could have no power;
   A virgin honour is a crystal tower
   Which being weak is guarded with good spirits:
   Until she basely yields no ill inherits.   155
GRATIANA
   Oh happy child! Faith and thy birth hath saved me.
   'Mongst thousand daughters happiest of all others!
   Be thou a glass for maids, and I for mothers.   *Exeunt*

---

133 *held* Q (child *conj. Collins*)
142–3 ed. (An ... sonne / Oh ... beggars Q)
150–1 ed. (*one line in* Q)
158 *glass* i.e., image of perfection (Compare *Hamlet* III. i. 153 'glass of fashion'.)
158 *Be* ed. (Buy Q)

[Act V, Scene i]

Enter VINDICE *and* HIPPOLITO [*with the duke's corpse*]

VINDICE
So, so, he leans well; take heed you wake him not brother.
HIPPOLITO
I warrant you, my life for yours.
VINDICE
That's a good lay, for I must kill myself! [*Points to corpse*]
Brother that's I: that sits for me: do you mark it. And I must
stand ready here to make away myself yonder; I must sit to   5
be killed, and stand to kill myself – I could vary it not so
little as thrice over again, 't'as some eight returns like
Michaelmas Term.
HIPPOLITO
That's enow, o' conscience.
VINDICE
But sirrah does the duke's son come single?   10
HIPPOLITO
No, there's the hell on't, his faith's too feeble to go alone.
He brings flesh-flies after him that will buzz against supper
time, and hum for his coming out.
VINDICE
Ah the fly-flop of vengeance beat 'em to pieces! Here was
the sweetest occasion, the fittest hour to have made my   15
revenge familiar with him – shown him the body of the
duke his father, and how quaintly he died like a politician in
hugger-mugger – made no man acquainted with it, and in
catastrophe slain him over his father's breast! And oh I'm
mad to lose such a sweet opportunity.   20

---

0 sd The corpse is arranged as if asleep, as lines 42–3 indicate. Macabre comedy
  was made, in the 1988 Swan Theatre production, of the fact that rigor mortis
  had set in and the corpse was far from pliant.

3 *lay* bet

7 *returns* i.e., various ways of describing it. A return, technically speaking, was a
  report on a writ or court order: hence, *returns* meant also the days such reports
  were made. Michaelmas term had eight such days (Foakes).

12 *flesh-flies* Hamlet calls the sycophantic courtier Osric a 'water-fly' (*Hamlet*
  V. ii. 82). Flesh-flies lay their eggs in putrefying flesh, and hence serve as
  metaphors for those who live off court corruption.

16 *shown* ed. (show Q). The past tense is required following 'to have made', and
  note line 18's *slain*, which is part of the same construction.

17 *died* Q corrected (did Q uncorrected)
  like . . . hugger-mugger i.e., like a machiavel in some secret intrigue. See *Hamlet*
  IV. v. 83–4: 'we have done but greenly/In hugger-mugger to inter him'.

HIPPOLITO
Nay push, prithee be content! There's no remedy present;
may not hereafter times open in as fair faces as this?
VINDICE
They may if they can paint so well.
HIPPOLITO
Come now, to avoid all suspicion let's forsake this room
and be going to meet the duke's son.   25
VINDICE
Content, I'm for any weather. Heart, step close, here he
comes!

Enter LUSSURIOSO

HIPPOLITO
My honoured lord.
LUSSURIOSO
Oh me – you both present.
VINDICE
E'en newly my lord, just as your lordship entered now.   30
About this place we had notice given he should be, but in
some loathsome plight or other.
HIPPOLITO
Came your honour private?
LUSSURIOSO
Private enough for this: only a few
Attend my coming out.
HIPPOLITO [*Aside*]   Death rot those few!   35
LUSSURIOSO
Stay – yonder's the slave.
VINDICE
Mass there's the slave indeed my lord.
[*Aside*] 'Tis a good child, he calls his father slave!
LUSSURIOSO
Ay, that's the villain, the damned villain! Softly,
Tread easy.
VINDICE   Puh, I warrant you my lord,   40
We'll stifle in our breaths.
LUSSURIOSO   That will do well.
Base rogue thou sleepest thy last! [*Aside*] 'Tis policy
To have him killed in's sleep, for if he waked
He would betray all to them.
VINDICE   But my lord –

23 *paint* i.e., use face-paint: see IV. ii. 221–2 and n.
40 *Puh* Q (Push *Harrier*)
40–41 ed. (Tread easy / Puh . . . breaths / That . . . well / Q)

LUSSURIOSO
  Ha? What say'st?   45
VINDICE
  Shall we kill him now he's drunk?
LUSSURIOSO   Ay, best of all.
VINDICE
  Why then he will ne'er live to be sober.
LUSSURIOSO
  No matter: let him reel to hell.
VINDICE
  But being so full of liquor I fear he will put out all the fire!
LUSSURIOSO
  Thou art a mad breast!   50
VINDICE
  [*Aside*] And leave none to warm your lordship's gols
  withall. – For he that dies drunk falls into hell fire like a
  bucket o' water: qush, qush.
LUSSURIOSO
  Come, be ready, nake your swords, think of your wrongs:
  this slave has injured you.   55
VINDICE
  Troth so he has, and he has paid well for't.
LUSSURIOSO
  Meet with him now.
VINDICE
  You'll bear us out my lord?
LUSSURIOSO
  Puh, am I a lord for nothing think you? Quickly now!
VINDICE
  Sa, sa, sa, thump! [*He stabs the corpse*] There he lies!   60
LUSSURIOSO
  Nimbly done. [*Approaches the corpse*] Ha! Oh, villains,
    murderers,
  'Tis the old duke my father!
VINDICE [*Aside*]   That's a jest.
LUSSURIOSO
  What, stiff and cold already?
  Oh pardon me to call you from your names,

46 Recalling *Hamlet* III. ii. 84–92.
50 *breast* Q corrected (beast Q uncorrected)
51 *gols* hands
53 *qush* splash
54 *nake* Q corrected (make Q uncorrected) = unsheathe
58 *bear us out* support us
64 *from your names* far from what you deserve

'Tis none of your deed; that villain Piato   65
Whom you thought now to kill has murdered him
And left him thus disguised.
HIPPOLITO   And not unlikely.
VINDICE
  Oh rascal, was he not ashamed
  To put the duke into a greasy doublet?
LUSSURIOSO
  He has been cold and stiff – who knows how long?   70
VINDICE
  [*Aside*] Marry that do I!
LUSSURIOSO
  No words, I pray, of anything intended!
VINDICE
  Oh my lord.
HIPPOLITO
  I would fain have your lordship think that we have small
  reason to prate.   75
LUSSURIOSO
  Faith thou sayest true. I'll forthwith send to Court
  For all the nobles, bastard, duchess, all –
  How here by miracle we found him dead
  And, in his raiment, that foul villain fled.
VINDICE
  That will be the best way my lord, to clear us all; let's cast   80
  about to be clear.
LUSSURIOSO
  Ho! Nencio, Sordido, and the rest!

Enter all [*his attendants*]

1 ATTENDANT
  My lord.
2 ATTENDANT   My lord.
LUSSURIOSO
  Be witnesses of a strange spectacle.
  Choosing for private conference that sad room   85
  We found the duke my father 'gealed in blood.
1 ATTENDANT
  My lord the duke! Run, hie thee Nencio,
  Startle the Court by signifying so much.
                                               [*Exit* NENCIO]

86 *'gealed... blood* covered in congealed blood

VINDICE
  [*Aside*] Thus much by wit a deep revenger can:
  When murder's known, to be the clearest man.   90
  We're furthest off, and with as bold an eye
  Survey his body as the standers-by.
LUSSURIOSO
  My royal father, too basely let blood
  By a malevolent slave!
HIPPOLITO [*Aside*]   Hark!
  He calls thee slave again.
VINDICE [*Aside*]   H'as lost, he may!   95
LUSSURIOSO
  Oh sight, look hither, see, his lips are gnawn
  With poison!
VINDICE   How? His lips? By the Mass, they be!
LUSSURIOSO
  Oh villain – Oh rogue – Oh slave – Oh rascal!
HIPPOLITO
  [*Aside*] Oh good deceit! – He quits him with like terms.
1 VOICE WITHIN
  Where?   100
2 VOICE WITHIN
  Which way?

          [*Enter* AMBITIOSO *and* SUPERVACUO
                with nobles and gentlemen]

AMBITIOSO
  Over what roof hangs this prodigious comet
  In deadly fire?
LUSSURIOSO   Behold, behold my lords:
  The duke my father's murdered by a vassal
  That owes this habit, and here left disguised.   105

          [*Enter the* DUCHESS *and* SPURIO]

DUCHESS
  My lord and husband!
2 NOBLE   Reverend majesty.

  91 *furthest* Q (fordest)
  94–5 ed. (Harke … agen / H'as … may / Q)
  96–7 ed. (Oh … poyson / How … bee / Q)
102 *prodigious comet.* A commonplace in Elizabethan drama is the idea that
    commotions in the heavens presage doom; cf. *I Henry VI* I. i. 2–3:
        'Comets, importing change of times and states,
        Brandish your crystal tresses in the sky'.
103–5 *prose in* Q

1 NOBLE
  I have seen these clothes often attending on him.
VINDICE
  [*Aside*] That nobleman has been in the country, for he does
    not lie.
SUPERVACUO
  [*Aside*] Learn of our mother – let's dissemble too!
  I am glad he's vanished: so I hope are you?   110
AMBITIOSO
  [*Aside*] Ay, you may take my word for't.
SPURIO   Old dad dead?
  I, one of his cast sins will send the fates
  Most hearty commendations by his own son;
  I'll tug in the new stream till strength be done.
LUSSURIOSO
  Where be those two that did affirm to us   115
  My lord the duke was privately rid forth?
1 GENTLEMAN
  Oh pardon us my lords, he gave that charge
  Upon our lives, if he were missed at Court,
  To answer so. He rode not anywhere,
  We left him private with that fellow, here.   120
VINDICE
  [*Aside*] Confirmed.
LUSSURIOSO
  Oh heavens, that false charge was his death.
  Impudent beggars! Durst you to our face
  Maintain such a false answer? Bear him straight
  To execution.
1 GENTLEMAN   My lord!
LUSSURIOSO   Urge me no more.   125
  In this, the excuse may be called half the murder.
VINDICE
  [*Aside*] You've sentenced well.
LUSSURIOSO   Away, see it be done.
                         [*Exit* 1 GENTLEMAN *under guard*]
VINDICE
  [*Aside*] Could you not stick? See what confession doth.
  Who would not lie when men are hanged for truth?

105 *owes* owns
128 *stick* i.e., keep quiet

HIPPOLITO
  [*Aside*] Brother, how happy is our vengeance!
VINDICE [*Aside*]   Why, it hits   130
  Past the apprehension of indifferent wits.
LUSSURIOSO
  My lord let post horse be sent
  Into all places to entrap the villain.
VINDICE
  [*Aside*] Post horse! Ha ha.
1 NOBLE
  My lord we're something bold to know our duty.   135
  Your father's accidentally departed,
  The titles that were due to him meet you.
LUSSURIOSO
  Meet me? I'm not at leisure my good lord,
  I've many griefs to dispatch out o' the way. –
  [*Aside*] Welcome sweet titles! – Talk to me my lords   140
  Of sepulchres and mighty emperors' bones,
  That's thought for me.
VINDICE
  [*Aside*] So, one may see by this how foreign markets go:
  Courtiers have feet o' the nines and tongues o' the twelves:
  They flatter dukes, and dukes flatter themselves.   145
2 NOBLE
  My lord it is your shine must comfort us.
LUSSURIOSO
  Alas I shine in tears like the sun in April.
1 NOBLE
  You're now my lord's Grace.
LUSSURIOSO
  My lord's Grace? I perceive you'll have it so.
2 NOBLE
  'Tis but your own.   150
LUSSURIOSO
  Then heavens give me grace to be so.
VINDICE
  [*Aside*] He prays well for himself!
1 NOBLE   Madam all sorrows
  Must run their circles into joys; no doubt but time
  Will make the murderer bring forth himself.

130–2 ed. (Brother … vengeance / Why … wits / My … sent / Q)
143 ed. (So … this / How … goe / Q)
144 *feet … twelves* (flattering) tongues three sizes larger than their feet
146, 148, 150, 152, 155, 160 speech headings ed. (*Nob.* or *Nobl.* Q)

VINDICE

[*Aside*] He were an ass then i' faith!

1 NOBLE   In the mean season   155
Let us bethink the latest funeral honours
Due to the duke's cold body; and, withal,
Calling to memory our new happiness
Spread in his royal son, – lords, gentlemen,
Prepare for revels!

VINDICE [*Aside*]   Revels!

1 NOBLE   Time hath several falls: 160
Griefs lift up joys, feasts put down funerals.

LUSSURIOSO

Come then my lords, my favours to you all.
[*Aside*] The duchess is suspected foully bent;
I'll begin dukedom with her banishment.
                    Exeunt [LUSSURIOSO] *nobles and* DUCHESS

HIPPOLITO

[*Aside*] Revels.

VINDICE [*Aside*] Ay that's the word. We are firm yet: 165
Strike one strain more and then we crown our wit.
                              Exeunt [VINDICE *and* HIPPOLITO]

SPURIO

Well, have the fairest mark –
So said the duke when he begot me –
And if I miss his heart or near about
Then have at any – a bastard scorns to be out.   [*Exit*] 170

SUPERVACUO

Not'st thou that Spurio, brother?

AMBITIOSO

Yes I note him, to our shame.

SUPERVACUO

He shall not live: his hair shall not grow much longer. In
this time of revels tricks may be set afoot. Seest thou yon
new moon? It shall outlive the new duke by much: this   175
hand shall dispossess him: then we're mighty.
A masque is treason's licence: that build upon –
'Tis murder's best face, when a vizard's on!
                              Exit SUPERVACUO

160 *falls* changes or disguises (Nicoll)
166 sd ed. (*Exeu.* Bro. Q)
167–8 ed. (*one line in* Q)
177 *masque* An entertainment at feasts involving dance and face-masks and often
    disguise; sometimes simple in form and costume (as in *Romeo & Juliet* I. iv,
    where the gallants consider having a short prologue spoken by a Presenter
    before they perform their dance, which is intended as a surprise), sometimes, as

AMBITIOSO
  Is't so? 'Tis very good:
  And do you think to be duke then, kind brother?   180
  I'll see fair play: drop one, and there lies t'other.

                              Exit AMBITIOSO

[Act V, Scene ii]

Enter VINDICE *and* HIPPOLITO *with* PIERO *and other lords*

VINDICE
  My lords be all of music! Strike old griefs
  Into other countries
  That flow in too much milk and have faint livers,
  Not daring to stab home their discontents.
  Let our hid flames break out as fire, as lightning,   5
  To blast this villainous dukedom vexed with sin:
  Wind up your souls to their full height again.
PIERO
  How?
1 LORD   Which way?
3 LORD   Any way! Our wrongs are such,
  We cannot justly be revenged too much.
VINDICE
  You shall have all enough. Revels are toward,   10
  And those few nobles that have long suppressed you
  Are busied to the furnishing of a masque
  And do affect to make a pleasant tale on't.
  The masquing suits are fashioning; now comes in
  That which must glad us all: we to take pattern   15
  Of all those suits, the colour, trimming, fashion,

----

in the Jacobean court, highly elaborate in costume, scenery, music, and dance,
and having a dramatic text. Such masques would end in 'revels', a general dance.
The masques presented here are simple in form, though they might have been
lavishly dressed.
179 *'tis* ed. ('ts Q)
  1–2 ed. (*one line in* Q)
  3 *flow . . . milk* are effeminate
     have faint livers lack courage (The liver was believed to be the seat of passion
     and courage.)
  7 *wind up* brace yourselves for action (Foakes compares Marston, *Antonio's
     Revenge* IV. iii: 'wind up invention/Unto his highest bent'.)
  13 *affect* desire

E'en to an undistinguished hair almost.
Then entering first, observing the true form,
Within a strain or two we shall find leisure
To steal our swords out handsomely,   20
And when they think their pleasure sweet and good,
In midst of all their joys they shall sigh blood!
PIERO
Weightily, effectually!
3 LORD
Before the other maskers come –
VINDICE
We're gone, all done and past.   25
PIERO
But how for the duke's guard?
VINDICE   Let that alone:
By one and one their strengths shall be drunk down.
HIPPOLITO
There are five hundred gentlemen in the action
That will apply themselves and not stand idle.
PIERO
Oh let us hug your bosoms!
VINDICE   Come my lords,   30
Prepare for deeds, let other times have words.   *Exeunt*

17 *undistinguished hair* i.e., down to the smallest detail; 'to a hair'=to the smallest
   detail, 'undistinguished'=too small to pick out or distinguish
19 *strain or two* few bars of music
24 *the other* ed. (the tother Q)
27 i.e., they will be rendered powerless by being made drunk
28 *five hundred gentlemen* This good round figure gives an impression of a large
   political revulsion at corrupt rule. On the other hand it is an implausibly large
   number for such a small-scale secret operation as actually takes place, and
   Vindice's jesting allusion (at V. iii. 124) to incriminating them ('we could have
   nobles clipped') seems to imply a smallish number. Five hundred might have
   been expected to present the new ruler, Antonio, with a reason for showing their
   leader clemency, or alternatively for arranging at once for a mass execution.
   Perhaps the dramatist overlooked the implications of the number.

[Act V, Scene iii]

In a dumb show: the possessing of the young duke [LUSSURIOSO]
*with all his nobles; then sounding music, a furnished table is
brought forth, then enters* [LUSSURIOSO] *and his nobles to the
banquet. A blazing star appeareth.*

1 NOBLE
Many harmonious hours and choicest pleasures
Fill up the royal numbers of your years.
LUSSURIOSO
My lords we're pleased to thank you – though we know
'Tis but your duty now to wish it so.
1 NOBLE
That shine makes us all happy.   5
3 NOBLE
His Grace frowns?
2 NOBLE
Yet we must say he smiles.
1 NOBLE   I think we must.
LUSSURIOSO
[*Aside*] That foul incontinent duchess we have banished:
The bastard shall not live. After these revels
I'll begin strange ones: he and the stepsons   10
Shall pay their lives for the first subsidies;
We must not frown so soon, else 't'ad been now.
1 NOBLE
My gracious lord please you prepare for pleasure;
The masque is not far off.
LUSSURIOSO   We are for pleasure:

---

0 sd 1 *possessing* installation as duke. This is the first of two successive dumb-
shows; all exit after the first and re-enter for the second.
0 sd 3 [LUSSURIOSO] ed. (*the Duke* Q)
0 sd 4 *blazing star* Not referred to in the dialogue until line 16, so this could be an
anticipatory sd. However the star's appearance just as the banquet begins would
be aptly ominous and increase audience expectation.
5 *shine* i.e., warmth of ducal favour. If the blazing star is already visible to the
audience but not to the nobles, this would have an ironic effect.
11 *subsidies* penalties (used at the time to refer to financial grants to the king by
Parliament)
12 *else . . . now* otherwise I'd be doing it now (i.e., I must not show displeasure and
so forewarn my enemies)

Beshrew thee what art thou? Madest me start! 15
Thou hast committed treason! – A blazing star!
1 NOBLE
A blazing star! Oh where my lord?
LUSSURIOSO Spy out.
2 NOBLE
See see my lords, a wondrous dreadful one!
LUSSURIOSO
I am not pleased at that ill-knotted fire,
That bushing-flaring star. Am not I duke? 20
It should not quake me now. Had it appeared
Before it, I might then have justly feared:
But yet they say, whom art and learning weds,
When stars wear locks they threaten great men's heads.
Is it so? You are read my lords.
1 NOBLE May it please your Grace, 25
It shows great anger.
LUSSURIOSO That does not please our Grace.
2 NOBLE
Yet here's the comfort my lord: many times
When it seems most, it threatens farthest off.
LUSSURIOSO
Faith and I think so too.
1 NOBLE Beside my lord,
You're gracefully established with the loves 30
Of all your subjects; and for natural death,
I hope it will be threescore years a-coming.
LUSSURIOSO
True – no more but threescore years?
1 NOBLE
Fourscore I hope my lord.
2 NOBLE And fivescore I.
3 NOBLE
But 'tis my hope my lord you shall ne'er die. 35
LUSSURIOSO
Give me thy hand: these others I rebuke:

15 The line may be delivered so as to show that the blazing star is at first mistaken
   for a stage-effect connected to the masque (this seems exactly in the spirit of
   the dramatist's stagecraft).
20 *bushing* a term used of a comet's 'tail' (OED)
22 *Before it, I* Q ('it'=my installation as duke)
23 *wear locks* i.e., the shooting or falling is marked by fiery trails. For their
   ominous significance see V. i. 102 and n.
24 *wear* Q (were)
25 *read* learned, well-read

He that hopes so, is fittest for a duke.
Thou shalt sit next me. Take your places, lords,
We're ready now for sports, let 'em set on.
                              [*looks at blazing star*]
You thing! We shall forget you quite anon.   40
3 NOBLE
    I hear 'em coming my lord.

Enter the masque of revengers (*the two brothers* [VINDICE *and*
          HIPPOLITO] *and two lords more*)

LUSSURIOSO   Ah 'tis well!
    [*Aside*] Brothers, and bastard, you dance next in hell!

The revengers dance. At the end [*they*] *steal out their swords
and these four kill the four at the table, in their chairs. It
                              thunders*

VINDICE
    Mark; thunder! Dost know thy cue, thou big-voiced crier?
    Duke's groans are thunder's watchwords.
HIPPOLITO
    So my lords, you have enough.   45
VINDICE
    Come let's away – no lingering.
HIPPOLITO   Follow – go!
                              Exeunt [*all but* VINDICE]
VINDICE
    No power is angry when the lustful die:
    When thunder claps, heaven likes the tragedy.   *Exit*
LUSSURIOSO
    Oh, oh.

*Enter the other masque of intended murderers, stepsons
[*AMBITIOSO and* SUPERVACUO], *bastard* [SPURIO], *and a fourth
man coming in dancing.* [LUSSURIOSO] *recovers a little in voice
and groans, calls 'A guard! Treason!' at which they all start out
of their measure, and turning towards the table they find them
                    all to be murdered*

43 Compare Chettle, *The Tragedy of Hoffman* I. i, where Hoffman responds to
    thunder's insistent peals, demanding that he execute revenge: 'againe I come, I
    come, I come'.
43 ed. (Marke, Thunder / Dost . . . cryer / Q)
49 sd 4–5 *start . . . measure* break off their dance
    sd [LUSSURIOSO] ed. (*the Duke* Q)

SPURIO
   Whose groan was that?
LUSSURIOSO   Treason. A guard.   50
AMBITIOSO
   How now! All murdered!
SUPERVACUO   Murdered!
4 LORD
   And those his nobles?
AMBITIOSO   [*Aside*] Here's a labour saved:
   I thought to have sped him. 'Sblood – how came this?
[SUPERVACUO]
   Then I proclaim myself. Now I am duke.
AMBITIOSO
   Thou duke! Brother thou liest.
   [*stabs* SUPERVACUO]
SPURIO   Slave! So dost thou.   55
                                   [*stabs* AMBITIOSO]

4 LORD
   Base villain, hast thou slain my lord and master?
                                   [*stabs* SPURIO]

   Enter the first men [VINDICE, HIPPOLITO *and two lords*]

VINDICE
   Pistols, treason, murder, help, guard! My lord the duke!

   [*Enter* ANTONIO *and guard*]

HIPPOLITO
   Lay hold upon these traitors!
LUSSURIOSO
   Oh.
VINDICE
   Alas the duke is murdered.
HIPPOLITO   And the nobles.   60
VINDICE
   Surgeons, surgeons! – [*Aside*] heart, does he breathe so
      long?
ANTONIO
   A piteous tragedy, able to make
   An old man's eyes bloodshot.
LUSSURIOSO
   Oh.

   54 speech prefix [SUPERVACUO] ed. (*Spu.* Q)
   55 SPURIO Q (*Spu.*)
   58 *these* ed. (this Q)

VINDICE
  Look to my lord the duke. [*Aside*] A vengeance throttle
    him! – 65
  Confess thou murderous and unhallowed man,
  Didst thou kill all these?
4 LORD None but the bastard, I.
VINDICE
  How came the duke slain then?
4 LORD We found him so.
LUSSURIOSO
  Oh villain.
VINDICE
  Hark.
LUSSURIOSO Those in the masque did murder us. 70
VINDICE
  Law! You now sir:
  Oh marble impudence – will you confess now?
4 LORD
  'Sblood, 'tis all false!
ANTONIO Away with that foul monster
  Dipped in a prince's blood.
4 LORD Heart 'tis a lie.
ANTONIO
  Let him have bitter execution. [*Exit* 4 LORD *guarded*] 75
VINDICE
  [*Aside*] New marrow! No I cannot be expressed. –
  How fares my lord the duke?
LUSSURIOSO Farewell to all:
  He that climbs highest has the greatest fall.
  My tongue is out of office.
VINDICE Air, gentlemen, air. –
  [*Whispers*] Now thou'lt not prate on't, 'twas Vindice
    murdered thee! 80
LUSSURIOSO
  Oh.
VINDICE
  [*Whispers*] Murdered thy father!
LUSSURIOSO Oh.
VINDICE [*Whispers*] And I am he!
  Tell nobody. – [LUSSURIOSO *dies*] So, so. The duke's
    departed.
ANTONIO
  It was a deadly hand that wounded him;
  The rest, ambitious who should rule and sway
  After his death, were so made all away. 85

VINDICE
 My lord was unlikely.
HIPPOLITO   Now the hope
 Of Italy lies in your reverend years.
VINDICE
 Your hair will make the silver age again,
 When there was fewer, but more honest men.
ANTONIO
 The burden's weighty and will press age down: 90
 May I so rule that heaven may keep the crown.
VINDICE
 The rape of your good lady has been 'quited
 With death on death.
ANTONIO   Just is the law above.
 But of all things it puts me most to wonder
 How the old duke came murdered.
VINDICE   Oh my lord.   95
ANTONIO
 It was the strangeliest carried: I not heard of the like.
HIPPOLITO
 'Twas all done for the best my lord.
VINDICE
 All for your Grace's good. We may be bold
 To speak it now: 'twas somewhat wittily carried
 Though we say it. 'Twas we two murdered him!   100
ANTONIO
 You two?
VINDICE
 None else i' faith my lord. Nay 'twas well managed.
ANTONIO
 Lay hands upon those villains.
VINDICE   How? On us?
ANTONIO
 Bear 'em to speedy execution.
VINDICE
 Heart! Was't not for your good my lord?   105
ANTONIO
 My good! Away with 'em! Such an old man as he!
 You that would murder him would murder me!

 86 *unlikely* unpromising
 91 *may* ed. (nay Q)
 98–100 ed. (All . . . now / Twas . . . it / Twas . . . him / Q)
 104 *to* ed. (two Q)
 107 Thus Antonio provides an illustration of the general law propounded by
     Machiavelli: 'He who is the cause of another becoming powerful is ruined;

VINDICE
  Is't come about?
HIPPOLITO   'Sfoot brother you begun.
VINDICE
  May not we set as well as the duke's son?
  Thou hast no conscience: are we not revenged?   110
  Is there one enemy left alive amongst those?
  'Tis time to die when we are ourselves our foes.
  When murderers shut deeds close this curse does seal 'em:
  If none disclose 'em, they themselves reveal 'em!
  This murder might have slept in tongueless brass   115
  But for ourselves, and the world died an ass.
  Now I remember too, here was Piato
  Brought forth a knavish sentence once:
  No doubt – said he – but time
  Will make the murderer bring forth himself.   120
  'Tis well he died, he was a witch!
  And now my lord, since we are in for ever
  This work was ours, which else might have been slipped;
  And if we list we could have nobles clipped
  And go for less than beggars. But we hate   125
  To bleed so cowardly: we have enough –
  I' faith we're well – our mother turned, our sister true,
  We die after a nest of dukes! Adieu.
              Exeunt [VINDICE *and* HIPPOLITO *guarded*]
ANTONIO
  How subtly was that murder closed! Bear up
  Those tragic bodies; 'tis a heavy season.   130
  Pray heaven their blood may wash away all treason.
                    [*Exeunt omnes*]

FINIS

---

because that predominance has been brought about either by astuteness or else
by force, and both are distrusted by him who has been raised to power' – *The
Prince*, trans. W. K. Marriott (1908), ch. 3.
113 *murderers* ed. (murders Q)
118–19 ed (one line in Q)
121 *witch* Because, evidently, he could prophesy.
124 *nobles clipped* Punning on (i) the clipping of gold coins called 'nobles', (ii) the
beheading of noblemen who took part in the plot.
127 *turned* converted
129 *closed* disclosed
131 sd *Exeunt* ed. (Exit. Q)